EMPHASIS ART

A QUALITATIVE ART PROGRAM FOR THE ELEMENTARY SCHOOL

"Animals in the Jungle," a group mural by primary grade children. The background is composed of two 4' × 8' beaverboards painted with black latex. Black construction paper stapled to mattress box cardboard or bulletin board can also be used. Each youngster in class contributed one cut paper animal which was stapled to the background. Children who completed their work early created additional trees, shrubs, flowers, and birds.

EMPHASIS ART

THIRD EDITION

FRANK WACHOWIAK
University of Georgia

A QUALITATIVE ART PROGRAM FOR THE ELEMENTARY SCHOOL

Thomas Y. Crowell
HARPER & ROW, PUBLISHERS
New York   San Francisco   London

EMPHASIS ART: A Qualitative Art Program for the Elementary School, Third Edition

Copyright © 1977 by Harper & Row, Publishers, Inc.

Library of Congress Cataloging in Publication Data

Wachowiak, Frank.
    Emphasis art.

    Bibliography: p.
    Includes index.
    1.   Art—Study and teaching (Elementary)
I.   Title.
N350.W26   1977   372.5′044   76-40321
ISBN 0-690-00868-6

Book layout and color photography by Frank Wachowiak
Supplemental photography by Ted Ramsay, David Hodge, and W. Robert Nix

To children everywhere, who make the teaching of art a never-ending adventure; and to their teachers, who share in the wonder and discovery; and to my former students, now teachers of art, who were so generous in sharing the results of their teaching to make this book a reality.

CONTENTS

Preface ix

Chapter 1 **Introduction** 1

Chapter 2 **Fundamentals of Art: A Review** 11

Chapter 3 **Children and Their Environment** 23

Chapter 4 **The Teacher's Role** 29

Chapter 5 **Avenues to Motivation** 37

Some Motivational Resources 43

Chapter 6 **Continuity in Art Learning** 45

Ages Five, Six, and Seven: Grades One and Two 48

Ages Seven, Eight, and Nine: Grades Three and Four 54

Ages Nine, Ten, and Eleven: Grades Five and Six 61

Chapter 7 **Avenues to Art Appreciation** 68

Chapter 8 **A Program in Action** 73

Drawing the Figure 74
Drawing the Landscape 85
Drawing the Still Life 89
Drawing Animals 95
Painting with Tempera 101
Tempera-India Ink Batik 109
Murals 115
Crayon 119
Crayon Resist 123
Crayon Encaustic 127
Crayon Engraving 131
Multicrayon Engraving 135
Oil Pastel 139
Oil Pastel Resist 143
Collage 146
Tissue Paper Collage 150
Mosaics 154
Vegetable Prints 158

Facing page: *One of a series of developmental drawings in crayon on manila paper 12" × 18". A first grade child shows herself brushing her teeth and combing her hair at the same time and therefore she needs four eyes, two for one task and two for the other!* Above: *The author and one of his young charges in a Saturday art class.*

Glue Line Relief Prints 163
Collographs 166
Aluminum Foil Relief 173
Linoleum Prints 177
Clay 183
Plaster Relief 190
Sculpture 195
Constructions in Space 201
Box Sculpture 204
Masks 210

Appendix A **Children and Their Characteristics** 217

First and Second Graders (Ages Five, Six, and Seven) 217
Third and Fourth Graders (Ages Seven, Eight, and Nine) 218
Fifth and Sixth Graders (Ages Nine, Ten, and Eleven) 219

Appendix B **How Children Grow in Art** 220

First Grade Children (Ages Five and Six) 221
Second Grade Children (Ages Six and Seven) 222
Third and Fourth Grade Children (Ages Seven, Eight, and Nine) 223
Fifth and Sixth Grade Children (Ages Nine, Ten, and Eleven) 223

Appendix C **Recommended Readings** 224

Books for Children 224
Books for the Teacher 227

Appendix D **Audiovisual Aids** 228

Films 228
Color Reproduction Sources 230
Color Slide and Film Strip Sources 230
Film Distributors 231

Appendix E **Art Materials** 232

Expendable Materials 233
Nonexpendable Supplies, Tools 233
Some Practical Hints 233
Recycling Found Materials 234
Some Special Materials and Tools: Suggested Uses 236

Appendix F **Facilities for Art** 238

The Classroom as Art Room 238
Location 240
Space Allotment 240
Furniture 240
Storage 240
Cleanup Facilities 242
Display Facilities 242
Other Specifications 243
Special Equipment 243

Appendix G **Glossary** 244

Index 249

PREFACE

When *Emphasis Art* was conceived, the intention was to provide elementary school teachers with qualitative yet realistic art education guidelines and objectives, with practical but also imaginative art teaching strategies, and with evaluative criteria that could give purpose, structure, and continuity to art programs in the elementary schools.

The response of educators to both the first and second editions has been gratifyingly positive. Classroom and special art teachers, art consultants and curriculum coordinators, and university art education instructors seem to approve the book's clarity, its brevity, and its many vivid illustrations.

This third edition results from continuing study and research with elementary school children. The art teaching strategies, techniques, and evaluative procedures described are based on classroom experiences and on observations of outstanding elementary school art practices, both in this country and abroad.

The intent of the text has not been altered. What gave the earlier editions their qualitative character remains. The book still concerns itself with the adventures, the joys, the responsibilities, and sometimes the headaches of teaching art to children; with the strategic, guiding role of the teacher; with art projects based on aesthetic premises; and with those important recurring evaluative clues that can help the teacher identify and encourage the art in children's art.

The third edition describes new techniques and discoveries, such as aluminum foil relief printing and others. Also, nearly half of the visuals are new, and Chapter Six, "Continuity in Art Learning," has been reorganized to follow the child's development more

Above: The cover illustration "A Magic Garden" shown in process. Grade 2. Athens, Georgia.

closely. (For example, all techniques for children of the same age group are treated together.) The new chapter on art appreciation will be of interest to all teachers.

Emphasis Art is designed for elementary classroom teachers who want to enrich their art programs. It is also written for the college student in search of a candid and unequivocal blueprint for high caliber elementary art practices. In addition, it offers a straightforward description of a proven, practical program for veteran teachers who seek continuing challenges, new techniques, and classroom tested projects for their instructional repertoire.

The importance of the instructor's influence is emphasized throughout the text. A creative, confident teacher, with a love of children and a growing understanding of dynamic art and design concepts, is the prime catalyst in the development of a worthwhile art program. Constant planning, thinking, dreaming, loving, organizing, adapting, researching, experimenting, motivating, evaluating, and resource-building are the challenging and often enervating responsibilities of successful elementary school teaching today. The privilege, however, of sharing the contagious and magical exuberance of children as they search, discover, and create is worth many times the extra effort and concern the teachers bring to the classroom.

Children from the first through the sixth grade respond and grow in a program where art fundamentals and techniques are not left to chance but taught imaginatively, sequentially, and purposefully. The debate concerning process *versus* product is not a productive one. Perceptive teachers know that wherever and whenever the *process* of discovery and creation is founded on an appreciation and utilization of art and design principles, the *product* always reflects this understanding. Mounting evidence suggests that we have been sadly underestimating the expressive capacities of children, and, in too many instances, have not begun to tap their artistic potential.

The philosophy and strategy of guiding youngsters as they express themselves visually, described and documented in this book, is the hallmark of those schools where the *emphasis* is on *Art*, art as an adventure, as a flowering, and as a discipline with its own singular demands, unique core of learning, and incomparable rewards.

Whatever compelling aspects this text may possess is in no small measure due to the expressive magic of those children whose creations sparkle across the pages and to those creative teachers who help make the art class a dynamic, growing experience for them.

W. Robert Nix, Professor of Art, The University of Georgia, acted as photographic consultant. David Hodge, Professor of Art, University of Wisconsin-Oshkosh; Mary Hammond, Athens, Georgia: Baiba Kuntz, Evanston, Illinois; Carolyn Shapiro, Brookline, Massachusetts; and Jimmy Morris, Indianapolis, Indiana graciously provided illustrations of high caliber art projects created by youngsters in their classes. Masachi Shimono of Nihon Bunkyo Shuppan, publishers of *Arts and Crafts, A Handbook for Elementary School Children*, Osaka, Japan, gave kind permission to use additional visual material.

My very grateful acknowledgment goes to Theodore J. Ramsay, Professor of Art, University of Michigan, Ann Arbor, co-author of the first and second editions.

EMPHASIS ART

A QUALITATIVE ART PROGRAM FOR THE ELEMENTARY SCHOOL

1

INTRODUCTION

The teaching of art in the elementary school today is a richly rewarding and a highly fulfilling experience when it is done with conviction, purpose, planning, understanding, and love. It is a privilege, a revelation, and a joy to observe and guide children as they create in paint, crayon, pastel, clay, wood, yarn, cloth, paper, and found materials. Their imagination and inventiveness know no bounds; their designs and configurations are excitingly unpredictable. No wonder, then, that their intuitive, naive, visual expressions have entranced and even influenced such noted painters as Henri Matisse, Paul Klee, and Karel Appel. To observe children develop in drawing, painting, and constructing skills, to see them grow from year to year in their artistic expression, is to witness a most fascinating aspect of human individual growth. Yet these same youngsters, deprived of the guidance and encouragement of a sympathetic, knowledgeable teacher, may stay on the same creative plateau for years. Their store of visual resources, command of the vocabulary and language of art, and

understanding of line, shape, form, color, pattern, texture, design, and composition may remain static or even retrogress, leading eventually to discouragement, frustration, and apathy.

Enriched and stimulated by a teacher's varied and challenging motivations, children learn to see more, sense more, recall more, be more vitally aware of their expanding and changing environment, and consequently be able to express themselves visually with more confidence. The teacher of art in the elementary school can begin to talk very early to the young child about the exciting possibilities and wonders of design and color. Today's children are more inquisitive, more alert, and often more discerning than their predecessors. Primary school teachers may have to rely on simpler teaching strategies, providing more easily assimilated art terminology for the children, but they will soon discover that children understand quite readily the ideas of using dark and light or dull and bright colors for contrast, of creating big and little shapes for variety, of repeating a shape or color to

---

Inspiration for children's drawings is as near as the school door, the view from a classroom window, a butterfly collection shared. Encourage looking, imagining, and composing from the first grade on. Facing page: *Oil pastel on colored construction paper.*

Preliminary line drawing in school chalk. Children were encouraged to emphasize pattern, details, spirals, circles, and radiating lines, allowing parts of the background paper to show through to unify the composition. Cortona, Italy.

achieve pattern or unity, and of drawing things large to fill the page. It is the teacher's responsibility to help build the children's creative confidence by guiding them as they move from one art learning stage to another toward the attainment of discriminating design awareness, repeating when necessary those art principles and design components that can bolster their visual expression and give purpose to their performance.

Teachers have been misled too often by the false assumption that anything a child draws, paints, or constructs is *art*. It may be, indeed, a child's visual statement, but it is not necessarily a work of art. To be art, it must, as far as possible, be expressed in the language, structure, and form of art. Children who express their responses, their ideas, and their reactions with honesty and sensitivity in a framework of compositional design create *art*. For the majority of children this sense of design, of art structure, and of aesthetic form must come from the many planned art-life experiences and happenings provided by the teacher. This knowledge can be augmented and reinforced by visits to art centers and museums and by exposure to choice art books, reproductions, films, and periodicals (see Appendixes C and D).

Very often what some observers call art in a child's drawing is not art at all but simply a visual statement that relates more to elementary writing. Art, on the other hand, is more akin to poetry, which, approximating fine art, comes to life when it distills the essence of things in highly expressive and discriminative choices. A basic statement, such as "I live in a house," might be compared, for example, to a stereo-

These paintings by children around the world show that they were not content with stereotyped, shorthand versions of a place or event. They combined perception and recall with art skills to document their experiences vividly. Top: Hong Kong; Center: Manila; Bottom: Taipei.

typed drawing of a boxlike house in the middle of a page. If we asked a young child to tell us where he lives in a poetic way, he might say:

My house is sunny white with a red tile roof.
It peeks through two big willow trees
And a blue door in front says, "Come in."

A green bush hedge makes a circle around my house,
And red and yellow tulips hug the porch
Where I sit on a swing and say, "Come in."

In much the same manner, poetic style enlivens and enriches the children's visual expression as they call upon their store of perception, awareness, and

---

Children all around the world respond to similar environmental motivations for the themes and subject matter of their art. Their creative, artistic endeavors are influenced by their culture, their nation's stature and values, family structure, education, religion, geographic location, economics, and political climate. In this painting by a young Greek child, he tells us all he has learned about his world. We see it through his eyes—the sea, ship, village, mountain, winding road, forest, orchards, harvesters, and, of course, the wonderful, warm sun that appears as if by magic in almost every young child's painting. Long may it shine!

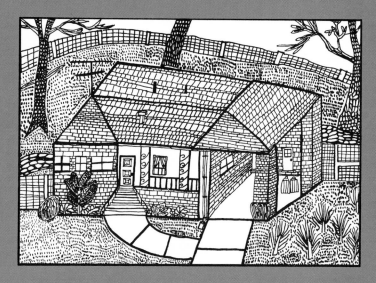

eidetic imagery for their drawing. The house then changes from the common boxlike stereotype in the middle of the page to a highly personal place, individual and unique. It may be a house of textured brick, rough stone, clapboard, redwood, cedar shingles, or cast cement, with chimneys, shutters, iron railings, breezeways, carports, windvanes, trellises, creeping vines, lantern posts, picture windows, rock gardens, pierced screens, television antennas, molded cornices, picket fences, window flower boxes, winding driveways, cobblestoned walks, or sculptured hedges.

In poetry, we discover that the quality of the interpretation often depends on the choice utilization of an expressive word, phrase, or couplet, on effective alliteration, on accent, on meter or rhythm, and sometimes on rhyme. In the most evocative, the most colorful art creations of children, one discerns a corollary employment of art principles and fundamentals resulting in a unity and expressive design that distinguishes them from the ordinary, often impoverished, statement.

In practically every art guide we find an emphasis on the teacher's responsibility to help youngsters engage in worthwhile experiences in order that they may have something meaningful to express, draw, paint, print, sculpt, or construct. Sometimes we find them helping the children recall a past event or impression. More often they provide new visual enrichments through a field trip, a model brought to class, a dramatization, a film, a dance, a musical recording, a story, or a poem. But for qualitative teaching in art, this initial stimulation is not enough.

Children who are challenged to a keen awareness of their environment and encouraged to be "noticers" draw their homes in a personal, individual way emphasizing those features that make them different and unique. Upper grade youngsters devoted at least 2 hours to the drawings on this page.

The teacher must also learn to guide and to counsel the children as they continue their creations, helping them to express their reactions and their responses in a growing, artistic framework.

Every time children create a work of art, a painting, a collage, a print, or a sculpture they should be encouraged to evaluate their effort from stage to stage in the creative process, always beginning with the initial drawing. If nothing is said to the growing youngsters about design, structure, composition, line, value, color, texture, pattern, and other aspects of the visual art form, it is presumptuous to assume they will develop in aesthetic awareness and artistic potential.

We are surfeited with the reassurances of well-meaning art educators and early childhood psychologists who insist that it is easy to teach art to children. They speak of "the relatively little effort required" or tell us that "to be creative, children need only materials and a place to work."

Let's keep the records straight! Art is not easy to teach; that is, if we are speaking about a bona fide art class and not a play session. Teaching art requires as much preparation, intelligence, and organizational skill as any other subject area in the school and, in certain instances, even more. The teacher's confidence and expertise is a major factor in the initiation and implementation of a quality art program.

Children who persist as they draw, paint, print, and construct will create more fulfilling, more exciting art when they are guided to see more, to notice more, and to become more aware of their environment. If their contact with the world, with people, and with

The cat is a favorite drawing subject for young children. Here children used oil pastel over a preliminary felt-nib pen drawing to depict cats frolicking in a garden. Many colorful photos of cats and flowers were introduced for visual enrichment and motivation.

nature is superficial, if they only half-see life's possibilities, if their identification with the visual stimulus is minimal, then they are apt to be content with a casual, noncommitted shorthand statement of an experience or event. Stereotyped interpretations such as stick figures, lollypop trees, square houses with triangle roofs, two ovals for a cat's body, or two curved lines for a bird in flight, are seldom based on a truly perceived, richly observed experience.

The art teacher must be constantly resourceful, prepared to help the child respond more fully, react more sensitively, and distinguish identifying characteristics more readily and effectively. This aspect of teacher guidance is only one part of the complex job of motivation, but without it, the average child's visual expressions tend to be cursory and sterile.

Teachers are often cautioned against imposing adult standards on children's expressive efforts, an admonition that is justifiable and commendable. However, there are some important standards based on aesthetic considerations that the teacher can and should use as valid evaluative criteria. These have to do with design and compositional factors and with basic art structure concepts. They range from simple, easily understood guidelines in the primary grades to complex and challenging injunctions for the upper grades (see Chapter 6).

Qualitative art experiences should have an undisputed and significant place in the total curriculum of the elementary school. When art is not allowed sufficient time in the school's schedule, when it plays a subordinate role to every other subject in the classroom and consists mainly of peripheral art activi-

Guide the children to turn often to nature and her myriad shapes, forms, patterns, textures, and colors for continuous inspiration in their art. Nowhere else are the elements of variety within unity so constantly and beautifully exemplified.

ties such as chart or map making, stereotyped holiday decorations, and endless posters, it is presumptuous to expect it to perform a vital role in the expressive, personal growth of each child. Art in the elementary school is justified as long as it contributes effectively and purposefully to the aesthetic, perceptive, discriminative, and creative growth of every child. Art taught effectively has a body of knowledge and skills to be mastered. It has unquestioned merit as a unique avenue to mental, social, and individual growth through creative action, and should be recognized and welcomed as a living, learning experience in its own right.

An unfortunate handicap in the implementation of a quality elementary art program is the continued employment of duplicated patterns and of misguided correlation practices wherein art is used to make the other school subjects more palatable. In this process, however, though the other disciplines may benefit, the child's love for creative, expressive art can be easily jeopardized.

Reports of art lessons and projects in art education periodicals often lead a reader to believe that teachers of the art lesson are afraid to voice their true convictions, to admit that they are influencing the students in their classrooms. Yet any intelligent, perceptive, and experienced school teacher can ascertain after observing the products of child art, either in an exhibit or as illustrations in a publication, whether an instructor's creative, guiding hand was at work, no matter how many times the article or exhibit brochure insists that the children themselves made all the decisions and all the choices. It is unfortunate,

Underwater themes employing the imagination intrigued the Japanese children who painted these fantastic interpretations of undersea exploration and adventure. When youngsters in school are capable of producing such rich visual statements, why do teachers so often allow them to settle for quickie copouts and stereotypes?

indeed, that so many teachers of art classes in our schools today are afraid to say "I teach!" Art does have content; it has a vocabulary, a language, and a history. Let's teach it!

Unless a person has actually instructed a class of 30 or more children in today's rapidly changing schools, it is almost impossible to say what can or cannot be accomplished in art. Frequently we hear from professors long absent from today's elementary school environs advising teachers to "give the child materials and let him alone to create," "teach the child, not the subject," or "remember that it's the process not the product that is important." How easily these bromides roll off the tongue! Strange that we do not hear math, language, and science educators spouting such platitudes. Classroom teachers, however, need more than such generalizations today. They need specific help. Many teachers faced with today's overloaded classes and schedules do well indeed if they simply keep the youngsters in control. Permissive philosophies will not solve their problems. Teachers can maintain an effective, positive, and productive equilibrium in their classes as long as they

can bring the students to sense the purpose of the project, the satisfaction in the art endeavor, and the serious direction of the learning. When youngsters realize that they are not growing in art "know-how," or developing a mastery of art skills, processes, techniques, and knowledge, they lose interest. The critical problems of student and class control are compounded. An art class where the teacher "lets the child do as he pleases" is usually a class where a minimum of qualitative effort and substantive learning takes place.

Teachers of elementary art can learn much, of course, from specialists in related fields. Psychologists, behavioral researchers, sociologists, anthropologists, and curriculum coordinators can help them augment their teaching strategies but *ultimately it is the emphasis teachers put on "art" that matters, teaching it dynamically, conscientiously, and purposefully so that the children placed in their charge grow day by day, year by year, in awareness of life, sensitivity to their changing world, creative potential, the ability to make worthwhile aesthetic choices, and their appreciation of man's unique contribution to a richer life for all through art.*

The young child above absorbed in her work is using the felt-nib pens and markers now available in a wide range of colors and in either permanent or nonpermanent inks. Be sure these markers are capped after each art session to prevent them from drying out. One color can be used over another to create new exciting hues and patterns. Children make countless decisions as they compose, design, and paint: what shape, size, color, value, pattern, texture to choose? A unique learning experience!

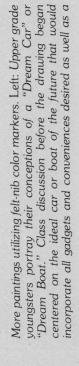

More paintings utilizing felt-nib color markers. Left: Upper grade youngsters portray their conceptions of a "Dream Car" or "Dream Boat." Class discussion before the drawing began centered on the ideal car or boat of the future that would incorporate all gadgets and conveniences desired as well as a colorful design. Right: Oil pastel paintings by children from Cortona, Camucia, and Terontola, Italy created in a summer art class taught by the author. The youngsters used the street market, family picnics, and life at home as the themes of their paintings.

"Which is Earth? No. 57." Ink and acrylic with collage on paper. Liu Kuo-Sung, 1970, 33½" × 23¼".

2

FUNDAMENTALS OF ART:
A REVIEW

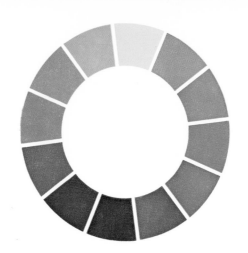

The teacher of art in the elementary school today is very often handicapped by a limited background in art fundamentals. A share of the blame for this deficiency rests with college or university art education instructors who allow their students to compromise, to settle for less than they are capable of achieving in art, and who permit them to dissipate valuable time and energy in stereotyped activities that call for little more than hand-and-eye dexterity or dictated step-by-step manipulation of tools and materials such as pattern-made crepe paper flowers, blot paintings, folded snowflake cutouts, and preschool fingerpainting activities. Another disservice is furnished the interning young teachers by instructors who encourage them to create in a childlike idiom employing child-oriented subject matter so that what often emerges in many college art methods courses are coy rabbits, candy-colored elves, and cartoon characters, everything, in fact, except the personal, mature, and sensitively observed images of the students themselves.

The qualitative, exemplary elementary-art-methods course, whether geared to the classroom teacher or to the special art teacher, should provide the student with aesthetically significant, high-caliber, and in-depth *art doing* and *art appreciating* experiences. Fundamentally valid art concepts and principles, based on recurring compositional factors in the visual arts, both past and present, should color and permeate the college or university art-education program. Its content should be characterized by a deliberate and continuing emphasis on sensitive and expressive drawing. Preliminary drawings evaluated in an art language should be the rule rather than the exception in the majority of studio projects. In essence, the students' inquisitive investigation of their environment, their continuing experimentation with new materials and techniques, their multisensual perceptual development, their self-identification with the natural order, and their often hidden artistic potential should be identified, encouraged, and rewarded at every possible stage.

This chapter is illustrated with the creative efforts of university students preparing to be art teachers and with the work of artist-teachers. It is vitally important that art teachers discover in college courses the rich potential of the tools and materials that their students will be using in elementary school art classes.

"The Shapes of Time: Iowa City." Collage employing found
materials. Ted Ramsay, 1964, 18″ × 24″. Collection of the author.

Teachers of art in our elementary schools can grow creatively and professionally if they continue to review and study the increasing number of fine publications on art and artists. As they read and assimilate contemporary writings on painting, sculpture, printmaking, and architecture, they will discover recurring references to the basic elements or components of art: point, line, shape, color, value, pattern, texture, form, and space. They will also find repeated references to art's fundamental principles or laws: balance, rhythm-repetition, variety, emphasis, dominance, subordination, radiation, and unity. Art, they will gradually discover, is a continuously challenging venture, a constantly changing odyssey with relatively few shortcuts to successful composition or good design, and although they may borrow ideas and inspiration from the rich past, they must reinterpret their findings in the context of the present. The future thrives on new approaches, new strategies and new techniques, it is true; yet there are some significant guideposts, some perennial avenues to design and composition which teachers can turn to in their search for a workable teaching strategy so they can confidently help the children in the art classes who rely on them.

Line in art is man's invention—the artist's unique method of perceiving and documenting his world. Therefore a primary concern of teachers of elementary art should be an understanding and implementation of the *linear image*. The line drawing is the basic structural network of all graphic composition. Expressive, sensitively drawn lines constantly vary in pressure, width, or emphasis. They can be delicate,

Dilapidated, weathered buildings, like aging men and women, often reveal a unique visual appearance that artists respond to. Here Ted Ramsay, Professor of Art, University of Michigan, Ann Arbor, captures the rich design "hidden" in a tenement cul-de-sac. In his preliminary sketch for the completed collage shown on *facing page, note how he deploys a variety of line and pattern while balancing his value masses. Observe, too, the subtle changes that have taken place in the transition from the drawing to the collage.*

bold, flowing, static, rhythmic, awkward, violent, or dynamic. They are achieved on occasion through freedom or spontaneity and, in other instances, through thoughtful and deliberate action. They may converge, radiate, parallel, meander, or intercept one another to create impact, tension, or chaos. An object, motif, or image is generally more visually exciting when delineated in a variety of sensitive lines. Lines expressively drawn can create and define shapes, values, and paths of motion. Turn to nature and man-made objects for limitless sources of line variety: frost, tree branches, spider webs, water ripples, veins in leaves, sea weed, wood grain, cracks in ice and mud, skeletons, bark of trees, insect wings, bird cages, kite lines, ski and ice skates, bicycle-wheel spokes, bridge spans, jet streams, road maps, tele-

phone and power lines, and TV antennas. Children in school should be afforded many opportunities to explore and express the possibilities of line in its myriad interpretations.

A study of pictorial design, of composition in painting, eventually centers on the *shape* of things. The shapes created by lines merging, intersecting, or touching each other take many forms. They may be square, rectangular, complex, round, oval, cellular, or amorphous. Shape can also be created in design by other means such as color washes, smudging, flowing ink, object printing, paper cutting, and assorted techniques. The achievement of varied, expressive shapes in a composition provides youngsters with one of art's greatest challenges and joys.

Nature is the richest source of inspiration for a

Note the effective use of asymmetrical balance in these figure compositions made by interning art teachers in the author's university classes. Class models are often employed. Left: Tem- *pera batik with colored tissue overlays; Center: Collage utilizing magazine ad cut-outs; Right: Oil pastel on colored construction paper.*

study of variety of shapes. Natural forms and shapes like those found in a tree branch, a leaf, a seashell, an egg, a cell, a pebble, a seed, a nut, a petal, or a feather are usually much more varied, more subtle than those based on mathematical formulas. Perhaps this is the reason landscape artists have often turned to dilapidated, aging buildings as inspiration for their compositions instead of the clinical and coldly geometric shapes of contemporary architecture. There is an illusive quality inherent in old things that gives them a special magic to the artist's eyes. To clarify this point, consider a utilitarian object such as a window blind. For purposes of function the slots in a blind must have similar dimensions and be spaced equally. But when contemporary artists draw the window blind as part of a composition, they invariably change the measured perfection of the rectangular slots to achieve more variety in shape against shape. They may alter the direction of the slots, omit some, or add others. They are using the artist's license to visually interpret the object in a more personal, more varied, and more expressive way.

There is far too much reliance in art classes on geometric formula and mathematical perfection in the rendition of table tops, cabinets, doors, windows, building facades, fences, sidewalks, and other utilitarian structures. Both teacher and students should turn more often to a contemplation of nature's multivaried forms when their own inventiveness in creating interesting shapes needs recharging.

The shapes of things or objects such as trees, animals, houses, vehicles, and people in a composition are sometimes called *positive* shapes or spaces.

The areas around them are often referred to as *negative* shapes or spaces, even though the negative space may include something definite such as sky, ground, or water. In any case, where the *positive shapes* are varied in size and shape, the *negative space* is invariably more varied and interesting. When a composition is effectively varied, it is usually "in good shape."

Value and the contrast produced by juxtaposing a variety of values play an important role in pictorial design. *Value*, simply stated, refers to the light and dark elements in a composition. Every shade (darkness) and tint (lightness) of every color or hue has a place on the value scale. Teachers and students must learn to perceive color in terms of its value in order to create effective and exciting color contrasts. Value analysis of famous paintings can help students understand effective dark and light orchestration and juxtaposition. Compositions with sharply contrasting values are usually dramatic and dynamic in theme. Less contrasting value relationships provide a tranquil, calm, and sometimes, a more unified interpretation. Value repetition can be utilized also to create movement in a painting and lead the viewer from one part of the picture to another.

Can you imagine a world without *color*? How dull it would be! *Color* basically has three properties: *hue*, the name of the color; *value*, the lightness or darkness of the color; and *intensity* (saturation), the brightness or dullness of the color. Yet its most wonderful property is often ignored. *Color has magic!*

Color in painting is a continuing challenge to art students, to teachers of art, and quite often to professional artists. It is not uncommon to see university art students perform with confidence when they draw or compose in black and white, yet find themselves completely frustrated when they tackle color. All the color theories, color wheels, and color schemes offered to date cannot help them, it seems, in their dilemma. The academic formulas no longer hold. For example, what were once identified as receding colors may now glow as advancing colors. Colors that simply "did not harmonize" according to traditionalists now are juxtaposed audaciously. Artists Henri Matisse, Pablo Picasso, and Hans Hofmann are acclaimed pioneers in liberating painting from local color renditions and restrictions. *Today almost anything goes in color—if it succeeds!*

To the elementary teacher of art, this state of affairs may suggest chaos and confusion in the realm of color orientation and color expression. Fortunately, there are still some concepts and practices that can lead students to an understanding of color, its limitations, and its possibilities.

In most colleges and universities studio art instructors suggest a possible palette of colors for their students, and although this palette may vary, it is similar in one respect—it is very often a limited color palette.

Limitation definitely plays an important role in the mastery of color composition. Sometimes art students are advised to limit their palette to black, white, gray, and one primary or secondary color, or to all the tints and shades of a single color as for example in a monochromatic scheme. A more complex, yet controlled orchestration involves the use of analogous or related colors, those adjacent to each other on the color wheel.

To avoid the pitfalls of clashing colors and strident chromatic relationships many art instructors recommend minimizing the intensity or saturation of colors used in a composition. This process, sometimes referred to as neutralization or dulling of a color, involves the mixing of complementary colors, those opposite each other on color wheel. Many colors now available in oil pastels, crayon, tempera, polymer, or oil are already neutralized; for example, sienna, umber, ochre, brown, chrome green, and sepia.

Even though many of the standard color theories have been questioned and even discarded, some successful strategies in color usage persist. A fraction of bright, intense color goes a long way in a chromatic composition that is basically neutral or soft-keyed. Colors may be repeated to create movement and unity, but it is recommended that size and shape of the repeated color be varied. Dark or cool colors usually recede; bright or warm colors generally advance. Complementary colors such as red and green in their fullest intensities create vibrant contrasts when juxtaposed. Black, white, and gray can be combined with any scheme without creating any tangible color conflicts. Often, as in the case of black accents, they may add the sparkle of sharp definition to a color design. Both teacher and student must always be aware that the character and impact of a color depends a great deal on the colors surrounding it; for example, a green shape on a blue-green background may be relatively unnoticed, but intense orange against an intense blue background will vibrate and arrest the eye.

The painters of the postimpressionistic and expressionistic era, including Wassily Kandinsky, Franz Marc, Karl Schmidt-Rottluff, and Odilon Redon, not to mention contemporary colorists such as Josef Albers, Karel Appel, Mark Rothko, Paul Wunderlich, and Paul Jenkins, have provided the art world with a whole new approach to color. No longer do artists rely on the use of local color which captures only the natural or surface appearance of things. A more personal, more subjective interpretation of color in its many aspects is now the painter's goal with resulting surprises such as blue horses, purple turtles, and green people. Painting today takes on a new exciting reality with an imaginative use of color.

Teachers and their students who wish to learn more about color and its expressive possibilities should study the paintings of the impressionists, postimpressionists, and abstract expressionists as well as the diverse, exciting, and sometimes shocking color manifestations of today. They should turn, too, for inspiration in using color to the luminous stained glass windows of Gothic cathedrals, the jewel-like miniatures of ancient India and Persia, the shimmering mosaics of Byzantium, the fascinating ukiyoe color woodcuts of Japan, and contemporary light boxes and color machines.

Space is an element in composition and design that can often confuse the young student. In two-dimensional expression, space is sometimes designated as the empty or negative areas between objects or positive forms. This kind of space is commonly referred to as decorative or flat space. Another category of space to be considered is space-in-depth, often described as plastic space. Common pictorial devices for achieving the illusion of space-in-depth on a two-dimensional plane as in a painting are: diminishing sizes of objects; sharp and clear details in foreground, with blurred, indistinct elements in the background; overlapping of shapes or forms; intense colors in foreground with neutral or dulled colors in background; and the effective utilization of traditional perspective principles such as vanishing points, horizon levels, and converging lines.

The elementary art teacher will discover that decorative exploitation of space is a natural expression for young children. The more objects or details they include in their pictures, the more intricate, varied, and exciting their negative space becomes. As they grow older, they discover other aspects of creating pictorial space through foreshortening and shading. Some of this feeling for space comes intuitively, but many children must be guided in the intricacies of perspective and space-in-depth. Rules of perspective should not be imposed on children unless they indicate a need for them. Students cannot underwrite the success of a painting by simply following the canons of perspective. Too strict a dependence on perspective formulas often leads to sterility in composition. The same compositional pitfalls await the student who relies too rigidly on natural lighting and on shadows or reflections to create solid forms on a two-dimensional plane. Teachers should encourage their students to explore interpretations other than those based solely on natural laws and effects.

Another avenue to successful picture making is the effective exploitation of *balance or symmetry*. Teachers and students should be familiar with the two types of balance: symmetrical or formal and asymmetrical or informal. Although formal balance was employed in many Renaissance paintings, the modern and contemporary artist has, for the most part, eschewed the rigid, static formulas of symmetrical juxtaposition. Purely formal composition, where objects on the right balance similar objects on the left, usually lack the open-ended orchestration and variety which encourages the viewer to look at a painting creatively, each time discovering some new avenue of approach to its appreciation, some subtle emphasis or hidden beauty.

A common misconception about composition in art is that *emphasis* can be achieved by making something very large and putting it in the center of the picture. Size and placement in the composition by themselves do not ensure domination. Other factors must be considered. If the motif or figure in the middle of the picture is simple in form, subdued in color, lacking in detail, pattern, or texture, and surrounded by brighter elements, then in all probability it will attract no more attention than a similarly treated object on the periphery of the composition. To achieve emphasis in a picture an object must have other attributes than centricity itself. It must, in fact, have eccentricity.

Despite the reminder that there are no hard and fast rules in composition, teachers and students usually discover that a pictorial design is much more interesting and more fluid when the principle subject or figure is not placed exactly in the center of the composition or page. As we study the works of contemporary painters, printmakers, and collagists, we are often made aware of the subtle and psychological utilization of asymmetry these artists employ. Although, at first glance, the key figure or shape appears formally centered, a closer investigation indicates a subtle shift off-center. In some instances where the central object dominates the composition, as in a flower study or figure portrait, the breakup of negative space on each side of the central axis is so varied that centricity poses no handicap.

Variety and diversity in composition have always played a significant role in the history of the visual arts. A study of the recurring aspects of variety within unity in great works of art, past and present, will be of inestimable value to the teacher of elementary art. Analyses of masterpieces of drawing, painting, and printmaking reveal the artist's reliance on and constant and conscious utilization of a variety of shapes and forms. Seldom does one discover two shapes in a composition that are exactly alike! Look at a score of multifigure compositions by recognized artists through the centuries and you will discover that no two heads are of the same level, no two figures are in the same position, and no two figures stand or rest on the same foreground plane.

Nature's wonders and its everchanging elements can provide inspiration with multiple evidences of unusual variety: ice floes breaking up on a river, the branches of roots and trees, the crystals in snowflakes, the cells in a honeycomb, the cracks in mud

flats, oil flowing on water, erosion in soil, snowdrift swirls, and the pattern of clouds. Though man is nature's child, unlike nature he must learn to employ subtle variety in his creative imagery. Too often the shapes he makes or invents are monotonous, sterile, mathematically restrictive, sadly conventional, and stereotyped. He might do well to look once more at the wings of a butterfly, the stripes on a zebra, the spots on a leopard, the feathers of a bird, the web of a spider, the scales of a fish, or the frost on a windowpane.

Variety as a force in pictorial design can be exploited in many ways in many instances. It can be employed in every element of a composition—line, shape, value, color pattern, texture—to give excitement and interest to a painting, but it must be used discriminatively and counterbalanced by a repetition of those art elements if unity is to be achieved. Emphasis, too, must be considered. Generally, the most successful compositions employ both major and minor areas of emphasis. The principle of variety can help students in the placement of objects, figures, or shapes in their compositions: these may begin on different planes, stop at different heights, terminate at the boundaries of the page, or overlap each other to create varied shapes and varied negative spaces between them.

The unified composition in which diverse lines,

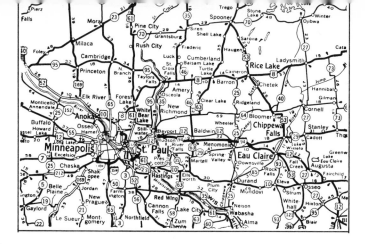

shapes, colors, values, and textures are incorporated or juxtaposed in an ordered yet flexible format should be the goal of both teachers and students. In too many instances, objects and figures are isolated in space, treated as separate vignettes. Often the figure, vase, animal, tree, or house is floating and lost in the middle of the page with no identification of spatial or environmental relationship. This pictorial limitation can usually be redeemed by the use of subordinate or overlapping shapes, through the repetition of an object or figure in varied sizes and positions, the utilization of related or complementary backgrounds, or the employment of environmental aspects that relate to the central theme.

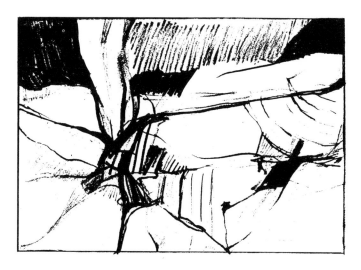

One effective method of achieving variety within unity in a composition and of breaking up the picture plane in a successful manner is to use the inspiration provided by a road map. Roads found on maps, in most instances, once followed the natural contours and delineations of land and waterways, so they are excellent examples of variety in line. Consequently, the shapes they create are beautifully organic and varied. In a map, as in a good composition, the eye moves directionally along the major highways or arterials with subordinate ventures along country roads. The areas circumscribed by the connecting and bisecting routes on a map can be compared in many instances to the varied, amorphic shapes found in abstract or nonobjective paintings. The observers enter the painting (map) at one of the many possible inroads, then are led to a major interstate highway that carries them to a point of emphasis or dominating center of interest (large city). Other subordinate

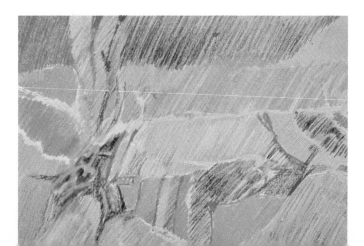

Examples illustrating the road map analogy described in this chapter. Top: A section of a road map; Center: The drawing based on the road map section; Bottom: Introduction of color. Oil pastel impressionistically applied on colored construction paper.

roads (lines) radiate, disperse, or branch from this focal spot to less important areas of emphasis (small towns and suburbs). The more complex the painting, the more avenues in and out of the composition are provided, thereby giving observers an opportunity to choose a different approach or entry each time they come to view the painting.

In this age of jets, rockets, computers, and moon landings it is indeed difficult for youngsters not to be caught up in the feverish rush of events. Perhaps that is the reason why so many art students race through their projects, indeed, why facile, instant, and minimal painting often appeals to them. Too much of what we see in art today reveals a lack of sustained, serious effort and learned skill. We are misled if we equate speed of execution with freedom of expression. A spontaneous, fresh quality in a work of art is not achieved easily. It is usually the result of many years spent mastering a technique, developing perceptive visual awareness, and integrating mind, heart, eye, and hand.

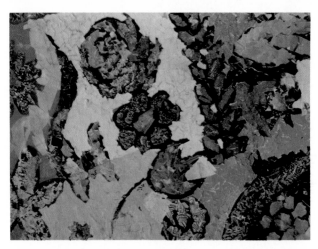

The basic art principles reviewed in this chapter are not new or improved formulas. Implemented wisely and consistently they can provide elementary art teachers with a realistic, workable foundation on which to build a qualitative school art program. There will always be exceptions to the rule, but in most instances and in most classrooms, a fundamentals approach based on a sound understanding and implementation of art's recurring elements and principles together with a respectful and growing appreciation of nature's infinite design will prove to be the most stabilizing and rewarding.

Some exciting collage possibilities. Top: *Cloth remnant collage on cardboard;* Middle: *Collage employing colored sections of magazines torn in small pieces and applied over colored construction paper;* Bottom: *Collage utilizing colored tissue and magazine ads over preliminary black ink drawing.*

"Animals in the Jungle." Oil pastel painting by third grade child. The teacher projected color slides of jungle animals on a screen and the class made their preliminary drawings in school chalk on colored construction paper. No two completed compositions were alike!

22

3

CHILDREN AND THEIR ENVIRONMENT

Children everywhere have much in common. They react in similar ways to their environment. They laugh and cry. They delight in seeing and manipulating bright, colorful objects and respond to sympathetic voices and loving hands.

Children the world over draw in almost the same manner at similar developmental stages, at corresponding age levels. They begin with haphazard scribbles, gradually acquire more control, then move to simple, geometric symbols, and finally to characteristic and semirealistic interpretations. Their natural

graphic responses are generally instinctive and intuitive, yet these basic representations do not necessarily mean that they are making artistic choices. What they express so spontaneously is usually done with an unconscious naivete.

No two children are exactly alike. Even twins, who may confuse their teachers with surface similarities, may have different personalities, different reactions and feelings, and different mental abilities. These individual, unique characteristics of children present teachers with some of their most critical guiding

Children often live in a special world half-way between make-believe and reality. Their art is the happy result of seeing, knowing, and imagining. The teacher can help youngsters grow in seeing and perceiving skills by providing a variety of visual stimulation. The teacher's sympathetic support is a crucial factor in the success children achieve in art. Indeed, the teacher is often the child's first critical audience. Be responsive! Be appreciative! Be understanding! Applaud! Above: Courtesy University of Georgia Museum of Art, Athens.

challenges. Teachers soon learn that they cannot expect the same responses, the same skills, or the same art interpretations from any two children, even those of identical ages.

Children in the same class may have diverse interests and different needs. They should be provided with opportunities to participate in a variety of art experiences or projects in order to achieve a rewarding measure of success in some particular technique. The youngster who excels in clay manipulation may respond less enthusiastically during the drawing and painting sessions. The child who confi-

dently tackles brush and paint may need more persuasion and guidance when faced with three-dimensional construction problems.

The fact that children are inquisitive and highly impressionable has been documented over and over again. They are susceptible to sight and sound influences every waking moment of their lives, yet are not always discriminative in their choices. Quite often the trite and tasteless element in their environment make as strong an impact on them as the aesthetic, well-designed product. It is a major responsibility of the teacher to guide the child toward more artistic

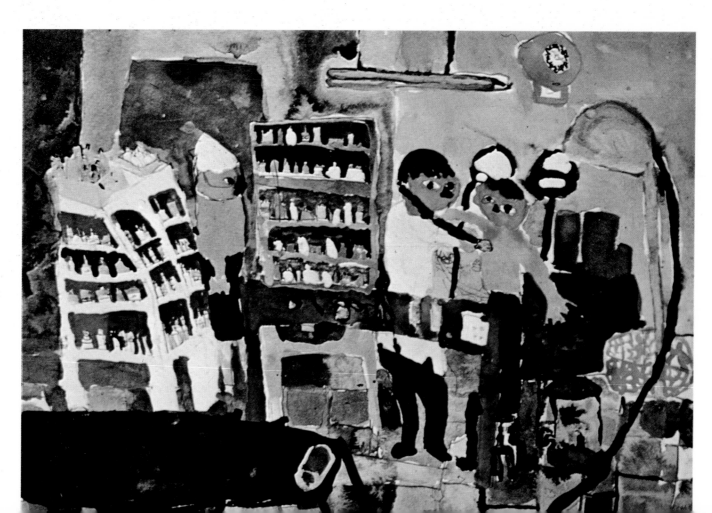

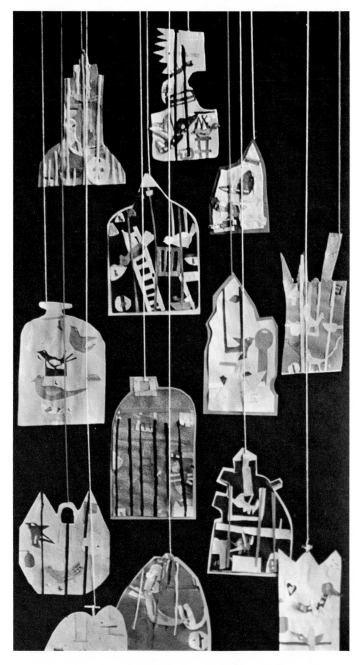

choices and to provide him with daily experiences to create and appreciate art. Children in school need the understanding, approbation, and guidance a sympathetic teacher provides, but they also thrive on the friendship, approval, spirited competition, and intellectual rivalry of their classmates. To grow, mature, and build their self-concept, children must possess a certain amount of security and self-confidence, an inquiring nature, and a stimulating, nurturing environment at home and at school.

Since no two children are like, it is impossible to categorize them by grade or by age. A teacher encounters a wide range of behavioral characteristics in any given grade. Youngsters in school may come from different backgrounds and may have had different experiences. Their problems and needs are not the same. Yet in order to understand them and help them grow through art, the teacher must be aware of those characteristics that have been identified with certain age groups by researchers in educational psychology, sociology, and child study. For a more detailed, more sequential description of children's growth and behavior, the reader is referred to Appendixes A and B. However, a word of caution is necessary at this point. The traits and characteristics described there are general clues to understanding children in general, and may not necessarily apply to a particular or individual child.

It is important that teachers have some understanding of the natural graphic abilities of the children in their classes in order to appreciate their developmental possibilities and limitations. The elementary art program that emphasizes quality, however, de-

Facing page: *What an impression "A Visit to the Doctor" must have made on this young Japanese child! How much he remembers and records! This page: First grade children made their own*

"Birds in a Cage" using colored construction paper. Yarn was used in the display.

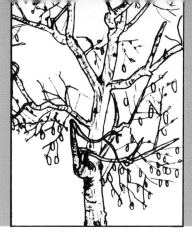

mands more of students than what they do naturally. It is true that a small fraction of children perceive, draw, and compose sensitively with a special skill in using line, color, pattern, texture, and space, but the majority of youngsters in the elementary schools today must be guided, stimulated, and persuaded toward richer utilization of design and compositional elements, toward a fuller awareness of their environment in its multiple aspects.

What do children really see? What do they respond to? What can they be invited to see, to feel, to hear, to identify with? If teachers can bring youngsters to notice something they have never noticed before, to see with the inner eye, they will have started the children on a rewarding, endless, exciting journey of discovery. The teacher can help children expand their horizons and visual repertoire by calling their attention to the thousand-and-one wonders in the world around them, such as:

> The intricate patterns of a spider's web
> The varied shapes caused by cracks in sidewalks, mudflats or ice floes

The subtle, pale colors in winter snow
The variety of grains in wood
The pattern of telephone wires criss-crossing a sky
The space breakup and design of a jungle gym
The muted colors of early spring farms and fields
The complex design of a honeycomb
The varieties of greens in summer foliage
The varied textures and patterns in tree bark
The shadows of tree branches against a wall or on the snow
The subtle shapes and colors of driftwood and autumn weeds
The graceful movements of a cat
The magnificent lines and tensions of bridges
The unusual cornices of historic buildings
The intriguing abstract designs of torn, deteriorated, outdoor billboards
The filigree pattern in leaves and insect wings
The variety and texture in stone walls and walks
The patterns of frost on a windowpane
The miracle of growing plants
The flaming colors of autumn leaves
The ever-changing formations of clouds
The dew on early morning flowers and grass
The reflections in water

No two children will draw the same tree in exactly the same way. The teacher's role is to encourage them to notice trees and their varied shapes: the trunk, bark, branches, leaves, roots, blos- *soms, fruit. Let them touch the tree, perhaps climb it, even pretend being a tree swaying in the wind, feeling the rain, the snow, and, of course, the warm sunlight.*

The moody colors of a foggy or rainy day
The flashing colors of stop lights, neon signs, beacons,
   and patrol cars
The rich luminosity of stained glass windows
The remarkable skeletal structure of man, animal, and
   plant
The subtle patina on aged metal or wood
The patterns of contoured farms and cities from the air
The oil slick patterns on harbor waters
The organic and varied shapes of rocks and pebbles
The subtle colors of moss on rock and stone
The color orchestrations in the sky at dawn and dusk
The shimmer of harvest wheat in the wind
The fiery smoke of foundries
The tracks of animals in the snow
The rhythmic and dynamic beauty of the ballet
The grace of a jet stream
The pattern of TV antennas against a metropolitan sky

Children are influenced daily by environmental factors which teachers cannot always control. Television, the press, radio, movies, the theater, musical recordings, store-window displays, magazine illustrations, paperback and record album covers, cars, clothes, and package design shape their developing taste and determine their cultural values. What a qualitative art program can do, in some measure, is to help the children be more selective, more discriminative, and more aesthetically sensitive in the many important choices they will make in their lives.

Many art teachers invest in a camera to take color slides of nature's store of wonders to share with their students. Their photo collections grow year by year and give added visual dimensions to their teaching. Color slides of varied subject matter are also available from several commercial sources. See Appendix D.

4
THE TEACHER'S ROLE

A creative, enthusiastic, imaginative, resourceful, adaptive, and sympathetic teacher is the essential catalyst, the *sine qua non* in the development and implementation of a qualitative program in elementary art. The teacher of the art class must be, among other things, an organizer, housekeeper, counselor, resource expediter, referee, adventurer, and last but not least, a lover of children.

Without a well-prepared and dedicated teacher at the helm, the art program may capsize in a stormy sea of hasty, last-minute decisions, in trite and instantaneous activities, or in chaotic, pseudotherapeutic play sessions. The school that boasts a fine physical plant, a rich materials budget, and an administration sympathetic to art, is fortunate, indeed, but if it does not attract teachers who are prepared to teach art confidently, creatively, developmentally, and qualitatively, then it has little chance of achieving and implementing an art program of promise and significance.

The reference to the teacher's dedication is deliberate. Dedication is, and always will be, a vital teaching asset in a democratic society. It transcends classroom expertise and management. Nothing is said, it is true, in the teacher's contract about dedication. Nor is there anything explicit in the agreement about the requisites of love, patience, and sympathetic understanding that go hand in hand with good teaching. Unselfish dedication and enthusiastic involvement, whenever and wherever they occur, are, in most instances, freewill gifts of a devoted teacher and cannot be measured except perhaps by the inner satisfaction and fulfillment they bring.

The best teachers of elementary art, whether classroom teacher or special art consultant, are creative, innovative, and adaptive people. They work hard to understand the basic premises, techniques, and evaluative processes of the creative act; they learn how to organize materials, tools, space, and time schedules to produce exemplary working condi-

---

Facing page: *The ever-renewing circle of life is all around us in exquisite and varied radiating forms. Teachers of art should turn to design in nature for constant inspiration and be alert to guide children to notice the subtle variations in the petals of flowers, the feathers of birds, the interstices of a spider's web, and the* scales of a fish. Teachers must be ready, too, to provide sympathetic understanding and support for children at critical moments in their art endeavors. Above in circle: *A child absorbed in one of nature's infinite designs. Photo courtesy Eastern Airlines.*

tions in classroom or art room, and they structure and implement the art program to meet the present and future needs of their students. They enrich the lives of their pupils through daily experiences in some phase of art discovery. They are constantly searching for ideas and art processes that can renew the children's interest in a project when the initial excitement wanes. In their enthusiasm, which they display unselfishly, they encourage the youngsters to open their eyes to the design, color, form, rhythm, texture, balance, and pattern in the world around them, in both natural and man-made wonders. They identify themselves with the students. They are excited and elated when a child makes a discovery or masters a skill. Conversely, they are genuinely concerned when a student encounters problems in his art endeavors.

Wise teachers plan the art discussion periods, the motivating question-and-answer session, or the preliminary show-and-tell segment with special care. They do not leave this important part of the art lesson to chance or last-minute inspiration. In many instances they prepare a written outline of their strategy. Because the time allotted to art in so many elementary schools is minimal, teachers must phrase their questions to elicit the richest responses in the shortest time. Their queries are usually the leading kind, seldom calling for one specific solution. They avoid dead end questions, posing instead, those that open up new avenues of discovery.

To keep the art program a vital growing part of the curriculum, teachers of art build and keep up to date as many art resources as they can: reproductions, photographs, color slides, film strips and loops, maga-

Drapery and crafted material from bazaars around the world, combined with old hats courtesy of a millinery shop going out of business, provide a colorful and challenging still-life arrangement for college art education classes. Two interpretations are shown: one cool and quiet, the other warm and vibrant.

zine articles and illustrations, recordings, illustrated art books, and examples of student art projects.

Teachers of child art develop expertise and confidence through continuous involvement with exciting art media and techniques. They experiment with the new materials and new processes now available in order to share them with their students. They do not assign a new project to the class before exploring its possibilities and its limitations on their own. The best teachers continue to search for new variations utilizing familiar art media, new approaches to student motivation, and new evaluative strategies in order to keep their own teaching interest and skills at a high level and to enrich themselves as vital, creative people.

Discriminative teachers of art learn to see differences as well as similarities in the graphic expression of children. They learn to build on these differences and similarities. They discover, if they are perceptive, that no two interpretations of a shared experience by the children will look exactly alike. In one instance they may find a bold, spontaneous approach; in another there may be a sensitive and delicate delineation. One child may be concerned with the intricate designs of pattern and texture, another might be fascinated by the fluidity of linear composition, and still another youngster may reveal an imaginative and sparkling sense of color.

A positive, cheerful, animated, and outgoing personality is a major asset for art teachers. In addition to developing a genuine interest in what the children are creating and discovering, they must learn, in sometimes difficult situations, to be patient, calm, and

The ever-changing art world provides new creative avenues to explore but often the older traditional crafts offer inspiration. Top: An interning elementary teacher took a clue from the San Blas Indian molas and, substituting colored felt, came up with a personal adaptation. Center: Yarn and cloth appliqué; Bottom: Yarn and felt appliqué.

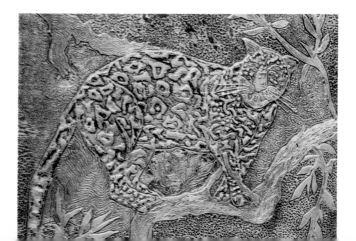

responsive to change. Children want to believe in their teacher. They need the security of a teacher's confidence in the subject being taught. Youngsters come to rely on their teachers for help with important choices, for possible resolutions to perplexing problems. They are skeptical of the teacher who confuses them with vague suggestions and generalizations, who places all the responsibility, all the decision making, in their hands.

Art teachers learn to listen to the child's description of his experiences, both real and imaginary, with genuine interest. They avoid a casual, noncommital approach. Instead, their excitement for the project-in-process is evident in their action, their words, and their eyes.

Successful teachers learn to cultivate a ready sense of humor. It can save many a disastrous situation. Teachers who really *care* about children avoid talking down to them and most important of all they do not underestimate the capabilities of any child or the child's potential to explore the everwidening horizons of art—its freedoms, disciplines, and rewards.

One result of the current confusion over objectives and goals in art education today is the false front so many art teachers are almost forced to assume in order to please all parties concerned. In too many instances, we find art teachers apologizing for making suggestions to children, initiating projects, and teaching art fundamentals and techniques. In order to win the approbation of the behaviorists, such statements as "the children decided" or "the students devised their own plans" are commonly used in articles describing classroom art projects. Let the truth be

The aluminum foil reliefs on this facing page are by university students majoring in art education. The process is described fully in the section on Aluminum Foil Reliefs. These reliefs exhibit the very rich and sophisticated effects that can be achieved with easily obtainable materials. A final embellishment may be added with gold Rub 'n' Buff paste or Treasure Gold.

known. Where exciting, colorful, successful, and dynamic elementary-art programs and practices exist, the classroom art teacher, or the special art teacher, is on the job—guiding, challenging, directing, stimulating, questioning, suggesting, approving, prompting, planning, coaching, advising, and organizing. In other words, *teaching*!

The initial strategies in teaching an art lesson are very crucial for its ultimate success. Projects introduced with adequate planning, with preliminary experimentation in the particular material or technique involved, and with exciting motivational resources on hand add immeasurably to the substance and continuity of the art program. Experienced and perceptive master teachers are quite often able to envisage the entire project or process with all its accompanying problems. This does not imply that they are not alert to innovative, unscheduled developments that may occur during the project. It does mean that they are continually aware of the broad and encompassing objectives of the lesson.

Another vital element in the planning of every art project is the housekeeping involved. The teacher must organize classroom facilities so that there will be adequate working space, a sufficient supply of materials and tools, adequate storage facilities for projects-in-process and completed, effective cleanup equipment and procedures, and accessible supply and demonstration stations. (See Appendixes E and F.)

Budgeting the time allotted to the art lesson is a very important factor. The children should never feel that they are being rushed through any phase of the project. Wise teachers carefully plan the amount of time needed for preliminary discussion and dialogue, for demonstrations and motivational presentations, for distribution and collection of materials and tools, and for classroom cleanup.

The most creative and most qualitative teaching approaches take a little more time, a little more preparation, and a little more concern for the needs of every student. Yet, teachers should realize that in many instances their young learners do not appreciate or enjoy a new art process or media until they become deeply involved in it. Once the youngsters see the possibilities in a technique or art material, their interest grows. This is why teachers must plan the introductory session of any new or difficult art project with care. If the art technique is strange to the children, the teacher can enlist the aid of the students in demonstrating the basic procedures, presenting the technical information in easily assimilated segments. Difficult steps should be repeated if necessary.

In a complex technique, it is advisable to have students explore or experiment with the specific materials or tools of the project before they engage in the final work. The teacher, too, should know which tools and techniques are best in order to guide the student in the process. Innovation and exploration of art media by the students should always be encouraged. For very young children simple procedures and techniques should be clearly explained.

The subject, content, or theme of the art project and its adaptability to the selected technique must always be taken into consideration by the teacher. It might prove frustrating for a student to make a preliminary sketch in fine pencil lines and then lose this detailed interpretation in the bold and heavy strokes of a chalk or tempera painting. The teacher must be ready to help the child relate his preliminary sketch or drawing to the final technique. For example, the utilization of brush and ink or a felt-nib marker as the initial sketching tool for a linoleum print composition is often recommended because both brush and ink and the blunt felt-nib relate to the strong lines produced by a linoleum gouge.

The teacher is the prime catalyst and bridge builder in the art classes. It is the teacher's responsibility to help build a learning climate in which purposeful endeavor, inquiry, individuality, and creativity thrive. When teachers of art are truly concerned about the expressive growth of the children in their classes, they plan and do things the youngsters may not always approve of. They may ask their pupils to set higher standards of performance for themselves or demand a little more effort than the children have been heretofore accustomed to making. They could very easily opt for a permissive approach and allow the youngsters to do what they please in art but, being concerned and conscientious, they continue to provide the highest creative challenges for their students.

Art teachers will find that their students can profit immensely if they use the chalkboard to outline the specific objectives or criteria for the project undertaken. In this manner the varied goals or possibilities are much more easily identified, and evaluations for the completed products can be more clearly defined. In the upper grades especially, these evaluative criteria written on chalkboard or bulletin board augment the teacher's effectiveness and are a ready checklist for the children, affording them the opportunity to make their own evaluation of work in process, thus minimizing their dependence on the teacher and discouraging the "Am I finished?" refrain.

Children in the primary grades who have difficulty in reading chalkboard instructions will benefit more by having the teacher simply discuss the objectives of the project with them, giving individual suggestions from time to time as they work.

Another vital requisite for a qualitative elementary art program is an atmosphere or climate conducive to the development of individual expression. Wise teachers allow children to work independently until they see that the youngsters are in need of further motivational fuel, then provide them with additional incentives to attain new levels of artistic growth.

A teacher's success in the art class is often based on the empathic rapport which should develop between instructor and students. The desired relationship may take a while to evolve but once teachers establish a climate of cooperation and of mutual understanding, their ability to guide and challenge their charges becomes the spearpoint or cutting edge of their teaching efficiency.

The special quality that distinguishes high-caliber teachers of art from the average instructor is their ability to respond intelligently, sympathetically, and purposefully to the children's creative, artistic efforts, to talk to children knowledgeably, sincerely, and honestly about their art work, to evaluate it, giving it importance and significance in the children's eyes by paying serious attention to it.

College and university students, preparing to teach elementary school art, should explore the varied art materials and techniques to build the confidence they need to guide the children's art endeavors. The illustrations on facing page are by students in the authors's art education studio courses. Left to right, beginning at the top: oil pastel resist, plaster relief, tempera batik, oil pastel, yarn collage, crayon engraving, crayon resist, box construction, and vegetable print.

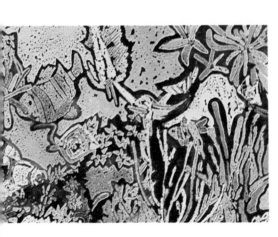
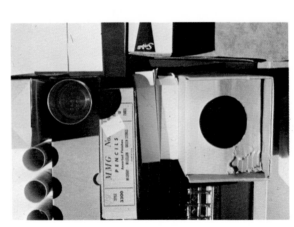

5

AVENUES TO MOTIVATION

Teachers everywhere agree that most children need some form of motivation, visual or otherwise, to achieve the richest satisfaction in their art. In almost every elementary school art textbook or guide published, repeated reference is made to the fact that children must have something to say before they can express it in visual form.

Inspiration for a youngster's art expression comes from many sources. It may spring from his experiences at school, home, or church; from his playground activities; from visits to museums, art galleries, fairs, zoos, gardens, national parks, shopping centers, circuses, parades, animal shows, races, sports, and games; from movies, television, theater, radio, books, comics, magazines, and musical recordings. The responsibility, however, for reactivating these motivational experiences, giving them a significance and an immediacy to trigger the youngster into art expression, is primarily the teacher's.

Teachers must be prepared to enrich the child's store of knowledge, to tap his recall powers. Specifically they might ask the youngster the leading questions *How? Who? What? Why? Where? When?* concerning an event or an experience. This avenue of questioning should be designed to encourage the child's seeing and perceiving, not just his verbal responding. The important consideration here is the development of awareness and visual discrimination. The teacher must be ready to help the child clarify and emphasize the significant aspects of the experience.

In many instances the teacher will find it necessary to provide the child with supplemental motivating material through planned field trips and varied vicarious experiences in the classroom itself. That is why teachers should have on hand or at close call a rich fund of audiovisual resources such as color slides, filmstrips, art films, examples of student work in

---

Facing page: *Inspiration for children's art is often as near as the school door. Teachers should take advantage of the immediate environment for subject matter inspiration. Here the children are using 18″ × 24″ lightweight cardboard or Upsonboard as sketch-* ing pads for drawing. Note in circle illustration above that the child shown drawing on facing page has now added an encompassing sun with rays that reach every flower in the garden!

varied techniques, color reproductions of paintings by established artists, musical recordings, and artifacts of all kinds.

The most vital art project motivations are based on vivid and meaningful personal experiences. Nothing replaces the actually perceived object or a direct contact for intense, immediate stimulation. Sketching trips to a farm, fire station, dairy, greenhouse, factory, or building site among others are recommended. Guest visits to the class by an athlete, a policeman, a nurse, an astronaut, a musician, a clown, or a dancer may sometimes be arranged to enrich the student's store of ideas. Live animals, birds, or pets brought to school will evoke stimulating and enthusiastic responses from the children that may trigger colorful art expression.

In the classroom or art room itself, the teacher can display nature's varied forms of fruit, vegetables, sea shells, seaweed, coral, driftwood, fossils, bark, mounted collections of insects, butterflies, rocks, gourds, minerals, live and dried plants, mounted birds or animals and fish in an aquarium. Still-life objects such as flowers, bottles, lanterns, clocks, musical instruments, lamps, and a variety of antique Americana can become the inspiration for many drawing and painting projects especially in the upper grades.

At every opportunity teachers should tactfully discourage the student's dependency on, or utilization of, visual stereotypes, cliches, or conventional shorthand symbols. They should minimize the "draw anything you want" assignments by emphasizing more drawing experiences based on things which can be immediately observed, touched, studied, explored, and felt.

Countless cultures around the world have created a variety of crafts and artifacts that can be introduced in class to whet the students' interest in art. Top: *Nōh mask from Japan.* Center: *Molas (reverse appliqué) from Panamanian San Blas Indians.* Bottom: *American Indian Kachina dolls and Navaho weaving.*

Teachers should help the children respond to nature and its wonders in many ways; they might call their attention, for example, to a butterfly in a pragmatic way by describing its biological phenomena, but, in addition, they should bring them to see its compositional structure as well, asking the children to use their artist's eye to observe the insect's design, the variety of colors, the pattern and textures, and the graceful shape of the butterfly's wings. This dual interpretation and description of nature in her myriad aspects should be encouraged in every art experience where natural and environmental forms are the source of the child's expression.

The materials, tools, and techniques of the various art projects can become motivating devices, too, and in many instances, may be the special catalyst that fires the student's efforts. In the primary grades the introduction of the new, vibrant pigments and colors in oil pastel, poster paint, crayon, and papers brings added excitement to coloring and painting. The free-flowing felt or nylon markers in assorted colors elicit an enthusiastic response from the youngsters in all grades. Tissue paper in a host of colors delights the upper-grade child who can handle it confidently as he discovers new colors through overlapping tissue over tissue.

In the upper grades, too, the teacher can whet the creative appetites of the youngsters by introducing them to melted crayon for encaustic painting, discarded tiles for mosaics, waxes and dyes for batiks, plaster for carving and bas reliefs, metals for casting, glazes for ceramics, and scrap wire, plastic, wood, and boxes for construction.

In recent years, critics of art education have called

attention to the proliferation of new media and techniques in the school art programs citing its deleterious effects. Though some of the criticism is justifiable, it is generally not the new materials themselves that are at the source of the problem, but the manner in which some teachers exploit them that is suspect. It is a known fact that a student with the newest, finest pigments and tools may produce a nonartistic, horrible work, whereas another student utilizing only discarded remnants from an attic, alley, or junk heap may create an object of singular beauty. The fault, to paraphrase a famous author, lies not in the materials themselves but in the expressive sensibilities of the creator.

The introductory phase of an art lesson or project should kindle the spark that ignites the interest of the youngsters. It is unfair to expect students to be challenged or excited by a series of art assignments or experiences that begin simply with the teacher saying, "Draw what you want today," or "Paint the way you feel." Elementary art teachers should devote as much time to the presentation of an art project as they give to the preparation of a math or science unit.

There are many effective ways to begin an art lesson. These include showing a film, filmstrip, or color slides on the project theme; viewing slides or examples of previous work in the same vein; guiding the class in a discussion of related experiences; conducting a field trip to enrich the students' knowledge of the subject matter; playing musical recordings or tapes to create the mood of the particular visual theme chosen; demonstrating the technical process with student participation; calling attention to a bulletin display prepared for the art project; introducing a special guest who might talk, perform, or model for the students; using selected poems, stories, songs, and instrumental music as project or subject matter stimulation.

With a varied arsenal of motivational procedures planned well in advance by the teacher, the student can look forward to the art class as a unique and rewarding period of the school day. Each project, technique, and age group demands its own pattern of motivation and only the teacher with a rich repertoire of ideas will be able to bring to the art program or art lesson the special ingredients that give it purposeful significance and excitement.

One of the most common problems the art teacher faces is the lagging of student interest once the initial excitement of a new project or technique has waned. This is especially true in those situations in which the youngsters do not set high enough standards for themselves and are satisfied with only a superficial effort, or for those instances in which the children do not develop a real concern for, or identification with, the subject matter involved.

There are always a number of children in an art class who find it difficult to persist. They complete their work sooner than the others, and feel they have exhausted the possibilities of the project while their classmates are still busily involved in their creations. This situation presents a real problem, because it involves an interpretation of the fine balance between what children can honestly accomplish in art with intelligent and sensitive guidance and what they are often willing to settle for. If at the outset of the project, the teacher, in collaboration with the students, sets up specific, understandable goals and criteria of achievement in technique, composition, structure, and design, then the recurring problem of children who rush through their work will not be such a critical one.

A criteria check list could be posted on chalkboard or bulletin board for the older students' reference as they work. Such a procedure could also alleviate one of the major quandaries facing the teacher, that of being able to guide each of the children effectively and still manage the multiple responsibilities of classroom management. When questions pertaining to the project arise, the teacher could clarify them with the entire class by pointing to specific objectives on the board, rather than repeating them for each student individually. Quite often work in progress by youngsters can be shown to the class with appropriate constructive criticism to emphasize the goals of the particular technique or project and to call attention to possible variations in expression. A suggestion given to one student will often trigger new ideas and possibilities for other students in class who may have reached a creative impasse or plateau.

At the upper-grade level the practice of writing brief constructive remarks on the back of the student's work, or on slips of paper attached to the youngster's projects, has proven beneficial in many instances and in a number of ways. It gives the teacher a chance to evaluate class work at a time relatively free of distractions and other responsibilities; it ensures the possibility that every student will receive specific, individual help at some time during the project; it

provides the youngster with a definite, working direction for each part of the ensuing art period that keeps him purposefully occupied while the teacher attends to routine tasks and special problems. This strategy for project evaluation, though time-consuming, can help the busy teacher implement individualized instruction, giving purpose and significance to the art program.

Another popular and successful method of renewing student interest in their art is to praise their creations which exhibit and illustrate quality design construction such as overall composition, sensitive line, innovative texture and pattern, effective space delineation, and vibrant color orchestration.

Because children can absorb or retain only a few ideas at one time, the teacher should not overwhelm them with an avalanche of suggestions. Motivation should be provided in small doses, introducing, if possible, a new and exciting attention-getter each time the art class meets. The following motivational resources are suggested as tried-and-tested possibilities:

Reproductions of paintings, sculpture, prints, and crafts that can supplement, illuminate, and intensify the objectives of the project.

Photographs in color or black and white that can extend the student's visual store of experiences.

Color slides of paintings, drawings, sculpture, prints, architecture, and sculpture crafts; design in nature and man-made objects; creative work by other children; work illustrating technical stages of a project; shots of people in action, in sports, and in costume; animals, birds, fish, and insects.

Filmstrips and cartridge tapes on art techniques, art history, and on correlated subject matter such as biology, anthropology, botany, ecology, geology, geography, travel, space exploration, and technology.

Films, TV films, and tapes that apply to a particular theme undertaken.

Books (stories, plays, poems, and biographies), periodicals, and pamphlets that can broaden the knowledge of both student and teacher and help bring a richer interpretation of the subject chosen.

Recordings (disk or tape) of: music; dramatizations and poetry; sounds of various geographic regions; city and country sounds; nature's forces; machines, ships, trains, and rockets; circuses and fairs.

Guest speakers, performers, and models such as astronauts, traffic officers, clowns, dancers, actors, scuba divers, pilots, athletes, singing groups, and musicians.

Resources and sketching trips to science and historical museums, art museums and galleries, artists' studios, farms, factories, wharves, airports, observatories, bus and railroad terminals, bridge sites, national parks, zoos, shopping centers, historical monuments, and boat marinas. (Be sure trips are planned in advance. Make a survey of the sketching site beforehand, if possible, to check on any hazards. Clear permission with the school principal early so that necessary travel arrangements can be made.)

Models for art class observation of drawing may include: live or mounted animals, birds, fish, flowers, and plant life, dried fall weeds, beehives, bird nests, insect or butterfly collections, fish in aquariums, terrariums, ant colonies, pets, skulls, rocks and pebbles, fossils, seaweed and seashells, and also assorted still-life material—fruit, vegetables, lanterns, kettles, vases, clocks, teapots, bottles, fish net, beach towels, burlap, bold patterned cloth remnants, and old lamps.

Artifacts from other cultures and countries, such as masks, carvings, containers, textiles, ceramics, toys, tools, icons, fetishes, dolls, puppets, and armor.

Examples of children's art work in varied media.

Demonstrations of art techniques by the teacher and students.

Constructive critiques by the students of art work in process with the positive guidance of the teacher.

Introduction of a new material or tool, or a new use for common materials or familiar tools.

Planned exhibits and bulletin-board displays that relate to the art project.

Introduction of an art design element or principle or a special emphasis on some compositional element, such as value, variety, texture, or color relationship.

Assorted objects and equipment to help expand the student's visual horizons: microscopes, prisms, kaleidoscopes, color-faceted eye-glasses, *touch-me* kinetics, *Magic Windows*, color machines, liquid light lamps, telescopes, microscopic projectors, and black light.

Strategic timing is of the utmost importance in successful motivation. The teacher must be able to sense when the children have reached a deadend or are fatigued and need stronger incentives to ensure progress in their work. The beginning of the class period is usually the best time to introduce new motivations, materials, and processes because the youngsters are most receptive then. The teacher should not interrupt a class busily engaged in their work to emphasize a point that could have been made at the outset of the lesson. Time allotments for motivational sessions should be wisely budgeted so that the children will not feel cheated out of their studio or activity period. The perceptive teacher learns through experience to gauge the listening alertness and interest span of the students, and plans the whole strategic sequence of motivation, discussion, demonstration, studio, and evaluation imaginatively, economically, and purposefully.

SOME MOTIVATIONAL RESOURCES

Teachers will find many occasions during the school year to use the following motivational resources and thereby enrich the art program.

Mounted birds, fish, animals
Acetate, celluloid, or Plexiglas sheets in various colors
New *day-glo* colors and papers
An aquarium of colorful, tropical fish
Ant farm or bee colony
Bells from the Far East
Colorful umbrellas
Duck decoys
Eskimo sculpture in soapstone or whalebone
Fish netting
Indian corn, hedge apples
Gourds, squash

Indian Kachina or Japanese kokeshi dolls
Magnifying glass
Window display mannequins
Masks: African, Mexican, Japanese No or Bugaku, Clown, Mardi Gras, Indian
Mexican, Indian pottery
Butterfly collections
Model cars and engines
Musical instruments
Navaho Indian rugs
Old-fashioned hats
Lanterns, clocks, old lamps
Bird cages and birds
Theatrical costumes and face make-up
Texture table
Puppets from various countries
Santos figures from New Mexico and the Philippines
Colored tissue paper
Spotlights
Full-length mirror, face mirrors
Japanese paper fish-kites
Glass fishing floats
Bicycles, motorcycles, helmets
Sports equipment
Multicolored glass containers
Assorted bottles
Stained glass
Cloth remnants
Wall paper sample books
Antique Americana
Contemporary posters, travel posters

6
CONTINUITY IN ART LEARNING

In no other subject area in the elementary school is continuity of learning so misunderstood and so poorly implemented as it is in art. Most classroom teachers are aware of sequential growth in other elementary school subjects such as math, science, and language and are familiar with the specific content and skills to be mastered in these disciplines by the children at each succeeding grade level. They can usually help the children build with confidence on previous years' learnings in these areas.

In elementary art classes, however, it is a different story. Teachers in the upper grades are often unfamiliar with the art program in the primary grades, if in fact, such a program exists. In too many schools art projects are a hodgepodge of spur-of-the-moment activities unrelated to each other or to the children's earlier art experiences. Too often these token art lessons are hastily concocted to fit into, but not to exceed the 30 or 45 minutes per week allotted to art.

Because there is a minimum of planning or programming of sequential art learnings, children from grade one are often fed a monotonous diet of endless crayon pictures, usually seat work assignments, to illustrate the various aspects of social studies, literature, and science. It is only natural for youngsters to become disinterested and bored when they realize they are not growing in new art skills and techniques.

Invite any elementary school principal or administrator to observe a class where art is taught *purposefully, seriously,* and *with emphasis on continuity of art learnings* and they will see education at its finest, a rich education of the whole child. They will witness children absorbed in making hundreds of decisions, sharing, evaluating, comparing, revising, selecting, and rejecting—all adding to their development as perceptive, discriminative, and aware human beings. Teachers have discovered that all subjects and disciplines in the elementary school benefit when art is taught purposefully. Children grow from year to year in confident self-expression and self-worth, in perceptive, visual literacy, and in the acquisition of a visual language.

Children express their ideas in direct, inimitable ways. Teachers can gently guide them to notice the multiple aspects of nature's designs around them, help them with special art techniques and processes when the need arises, and support them at critical stages, but what youngsters depict so honestly, naively, and boldly is often colored by a mystique that sometimes defies explanation. Notice, for example, in the crayon engraving on facing page, how economically and directly the child makes his statement about flowers and insects. In the circle illustration above, a youngster applies rich areas of crayon for his engraving.

The implementation of a sequential, qualitative art-learnings program in the early education of all children is of vital importance today. Art in the elementary schools is unfortunately becoming an endangered species because it wastes too much time on the insignificant, the peripheral, the "instant," and the stereotype. In many schools it is a kindergarten "happy hour." "All right, children," says the teacher at the close of an art activity, "put away your crayons now and let's get down to something serious." (Like math or science, perhaps?) It is no wonder that principals, administrators, and parents are questioning the validity and the worth of the art experience in the elementary schools; yet they are as much to blame as anyone when they settle for the unqualified and poorly prepared teacher and the unplanned, nonsequential program.

There are those in the art education profession who believe that the present smorgasboard of "quickie" studio projects should be replaced by art appreciation classes. They feel that a program of studies dealing with art criticism would salvage art in our elementary schools. I have found that art appreciation can be best implemented by a purposeful involvement in selective studio practices where art reproductions and slides are used to supplement and enrich the studio projects. One fact escapes the protagonists of the art appreciation theory. Children want and need to create, construct, and build! In all their other classes they sit and read, write, listen, and recite. How many times have teachers heard the children exclaim as they tumble into the art class, "What are we going to **do** in art today?"

Children should have the opportunity to sketch from live models brought to class such as dogs, cats, rabbits, birds in cages, turtles, and goldfish. Immediate motivation is usually the most effective, though mounted animals and birds provide an acceptable substitute in certain situations.

The solution, I firmly believe, is not to change the doing to talking and listening, but to *change from the present ineffectual direction to a more purposeful, substantive, and qualitative way of doing art.* That is precisely what this chapter is about; indeed, what this whole book is about. The following outline of a sequential, developmental art program is the culmination of 40 years of teaching and researching art at the elementary school level and of countless seminars involving thousands of classroom teachers, special art teachers, art consultants, and university art educators. It should prove of significant value to those elementary school classroom teachers who need practical and specific help in the planning of their art curriculum and should especially aid them in the critical area of art process and product evaluation. As you read the material in this chapter you can augment your understanding of it by referring to Appendix B.

The contour line technique is perhaps the most viable and successful drawing expression for upper grade children. Suggest that the youngsters draw in soft-lead pencil, slowly, deliberately, looking intently at what they are drawing. In some instances a felt-nib pen may be used instead of a pencil. The illustration above is a sensitive life study of her classmates by a Japanese upper grade youngster. Note in the drawing how every hair is delineated, how every line defines an important outer or inner contour.

AGES, FIVE, SIX, AND SEVEN:
GRADES ONE AND TWO

DRAWING, DESIGNING, PAINTING

Introduce the children to line, varied shapes, value (dark and light), color, and pattern. Encourage drawing based on personal experiences and observations but praise imaginative expression as well. Provide many opportunities to draw from real objects: plants in and around the school, animal pets brought to class, flower arrangements, classmates as figure drawing models, varied visual subject matter observed on field trips. Suggest drawing in large scale so details considered important can be introduced. Encourage the children to fill the page. In most instances, the more images or ideas youngsters incorporate in their compositions, the more interrelated and unified their drawings become. Discourage rushing and scribbling. Specific challenges such as "think as you draw" may be suggested at this stage.

One drawing and painting challenge that appeals to children everywhere in the world is the chance to create their very own imaginary monster which can be part animal, part bird, part insect, part fish, and part man! Shown on this page are make-believe beasts by children from Japan, the Philippines, and Hawaii.

The following rhyme provides clues young children can use to improve their compositions.

> Something big, something small
> Something short, something tall
> Something dark, something light
> Helps to make your drawing all right!

Introduce them to the various tools that make lines—crayon, pastel, pencil, pen, small brushes, a nail for crayon engraving, a stick in the sand, or a finger in wet paint. Promote discovery and utilization of varied line patterns—stripes, plaids, dots, circles, stars, radiating lines, spirals, scribbles, and zig-zag designs. Encourage observation of patterns in clothes, school and home furnishings, packaging and posters, and always in the wonders of nature.

COLOR AWARENESS

Begin teaching color awareness with emphasis on the child's everyday surroundings. Call the youngster's attention to the myriad of colors in their immediate environment: their clothes, books, and art materials and the paintings on display in the school. Help them to identify the warm, sunny colors such as yellow, orange, pink, and red and the usually happy events associated with them: the circus, fairs, harvest, picnics, and summer fun. Call attention also to the cool, deep colors of green, blue, and purple and the images they evoke: the mysterious night, the fathomless ocean, and the dark forest.

Build color knowledge with every project that utilizes crayon, pastel, paint, or colored paper. Identify the primary colors of red, yellow, and blue

Color exploitation projects. Top: *Painting in black enamel on glass with colored pieces of glass glued on back;* Center: *Strips of black construction paper pasted together to create motifs, colored tissue paper pasted on reverse;* Bottom: *Black construction paper with designs cut out with a razor, colored tissue paper pasted on reverse side. Put masking tape on single edge razor blade so only one small cutting point appears.*

and the secondary colors of orange, green, and violet (purple). Check records and files on the children for evidences of color blindness so you can ascertain their needs.

Take advantage of the many stimulating games, toys, and constructions commercially available to develop color awareness—the prism, the color wheel, and the kaleidoscope. Encourage color matching utilizing found materials and colored scraps of paper or cloth. Use a shoe box for each range of colors—blues of all tints and shades in one box, green in another, and so forth. Assign a cut-and-paste design limited to matching colors. Let children create colors by mingling watercolors or tempera on wet paper.

COLLAGE

Encourage youngsters in scissor-cutting skills and help them create simple shapes out of construction paper. Do you have scissors for children who are left-handed? Afford opportunities involving pasting little shapes of paper on big shapes. Point out how value and contrast are often created by pasting one shape over another, a dark color over a light color and vice versa. Offer suggestions on using and applying paste economically and effectively. In some instances the felt board can be employed to introduce children to the possibilities of cutout shapes of all sizes and colors and the many ways they can be juxtaposed and overlapped to create a composition. Cooperative mural projects in the cut-and-paste technique in which each child contributes one or more parts to the whole are very successful at this age level.

Recycle scraps of colored construction paper into collage projects such as these by primary grade youngsters. Children selected paper scraps in assorted sizes, shapes, and colors and arranged their compositions. Later, details, designs, patterns, and figures were added employing crayons, oil pastels, colored felt-nib markers, and sometimes brush and paint.

PRINTMAKING

Simple repeat prints resulting in colorful all over patterns can be made utilizing vegetables, found objects, clay pieces, erasers, cellulose scraps, and, of course, hands and fingers. In most instances colored construction paper is recommended for the background surface, although other possibilities are suggested: colored tissue, wallpaper samples, cloth remnants, newsprint, and brown wrapping paper. (See the section "Vegetable Prints" in Chapter 8.) Printmaking activities at this level are somewhat limited because the children do not possess the necessary skills for many complicated techniques. Brave teachers, however, are encouraged to try glue line prints and collographs, which are described in detail in Chapter 8.

CERAMICS

Provide one or two exploratory experiences with clay. It is important that sufficient clay be on hand (a ball of clay about the size of a grapefruit is recommended) and that it be of the proper plasticity—malleable, clean, not too moist, not too dry. Check the working condition of the clay a day or two before a clay project is undertaken, unless, of course, commercially prepared moist clay is used. Allow the children to discover the potential of the clay—encourage squeezing, pinching, poking, coil-making, and forming clay into pellets or balls.

Guide the youngsters in the creation of simple and familiar forms in clay. Suggest that they hold the ball or lump of clay in their hands as they manipulate it into the desired form. This procedure discourages the tendency of some children to pound the clay flat on their desk. Young children enjoy creating animals and birds in clay. They find that they can control the relatively simple sculptural forms of a rabbit, elephant, turtle, dog, cat, cow, bear, pig, hippo, horse, or nesting bird.

Children at this stage can also construct simple pinch pots. With a lump of clay the size of an orange they can manage a fairly successful container which may be bisque-fired if a kiln is available. The process is as follows: Ask them to hold the clay in the palm of one hand and insert the thumb of other hand in to the

middle of the clay ball. As they rotate the clay, they should push and pinch thumb and fingers along the inside and outside of the ball in overlapping pinches. Caution them not to make the wall and base of the pot too thin. The marks of their thumbs and fingers often add a natural texture. Remind them to avoid excessive use of water in moistening clay.

A GROWING ART VOCABULARY

Youngsters who grow in the vocabulary and language of art usually have more success in their art endeavors. Teachers should use all means at their disposal, including the chalkboard and bulletin board, to call the child's attention to the following project-related art words: balance, black, blue, bright, brush, cardboard, chalk, circle, clay, coil, color, construction paper, crayon, dark, design, dots, drawing, easel, engraving, fingerpaint, glue, green, gray, hammer, ink, kiln, light, line, manila paper, mobile, model, mural, nail, newsprint paper, orange, oval, overlapping, paste, pastel, pattern, pen, pencil, pin, pinch pot, plaid, purple, rectangle, red, repeat, ruler, saw, scribble, sculpture, shape, square, stripe, tagboard, tempera paint, texture, tissue paper, triangle, watercolor, weaving, white, yellow.

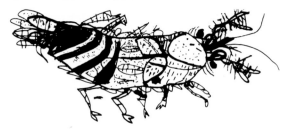

Vegetable printmaking appeals to youngsters but caution must be exercised in cutting the designs. Use nails, plastic knives, and melon scoops for making holes. Do not insist on a measured, rigidly controlled design. Vegetable prints may be embellished with application of oil pastels allowing some of the background to show and unify the composition.

SUGGESTED SUBJECTS OR THEMES FOR
CHILDREN'S ART PROJECTS AGES FIVE, SIX,
AND SEVEN: GRADES ONE AND TWO

Games on the Playground
Fun in the Snow
Picking Flowers in the Garden
Me and My Pet
The Wonderful Wild Animal World
Playing Ball
Skipping Rope
On the Jungle Gym
The Merry-Go-Round
The Circus Parade
Rabbits in a Hutch
Gophers at Home
The House Where I Live
Our Community Helpers
Butterflies in a Garden
Animals in the Zoo
Farm Animals
Animals and Their Young
The Toy Shop
Birds in a Tree
Fish in the Sea
Noah's Ark
Easter Parade
Every Leaf Is Different!
Here Comes the Clowns!
The Pet Show
Birds in a Cage
Land of Make-Believe
A Magic Forest
Over the Rainbow
The Jungle
Santa's Workshop

Top: *An example of the collograph technique which appeals to children at all grade levels. It involves cutting and tearing shapes of paper and adhering them to a cardboard or oak tag background to produce a printing plate. It is wise to cover the entire* *pasted composition with a coat of shellac to prevent the separate pasted pieces from coming off during the printing process. Use water-soluble printing ink and a "soft" rubber brayer or roller.* Bottom: *Linoleum print. Upper grades.*

AGES SEVEN, EIGHT, AND NINE: GRADES THREE AND FOUR

DRAWING, DESIGNING, PAINTING

Continue to call attention to the immediate and the visually stimulating subject or image for drawing. On sketching trips scout for the unusual, pictorially exciting vista. Choose landscapes and cityscapes with multifaceted structures and varied breakup of space. Suggest new avenues and possibilities in compositional structure, such as: overlapping shapes that create unity and subtle space; achieving distance through diminishing sizes and placement of objects higher on the page; creating pattern and texture as contrast to quiet areas; and drawing the line in a more sensitive way to achieve variety and emphasis.

Children at this stage can be introduced to basic contour-drawing techniques. For an immediate visual stimulus begin with simple, uncomplicated, everyday objects: a shoe, glove, bottle, helmet, baseball mitt, teapot, fruit, or vegetable. When the youngster's confidence in contour delineation increases, try a combined arrangement of several items, in some instances overlapping each other. It is very important that the children are guided to look carefully and intently at the object they are drawing and that they draw very slowly. Explain about beginning with the inner contour lines of an object such as the center petals of a flower, adding a petal at a time, instead of making a hasty general outline of the entire blossom.

A soft lead pencil is best for contour drawing.

A linoleum print by an upper grade youngster. Note how the composition fills the space and how strong textural effects are achieved by using the lino gouges in a rhythmic, directional manner. For a successful print, be careful that the children do not cut away too much of the block.

Erasures should be discouraged, if possible; instead, a second line may be drawn. The youngsters may stop at critical junctures of the contour line, reposition their drawing tool, and then continue drawing. The term *blind contour drawing* refers to the kind of drawing in which the students look at the object drawn but not at their paper as they draw. *Blind contour drawing* is generally recommended for the more mature child in the upper grades or middle school.

Continue to direct the child's attention to nature and to the variety of line, shape, texture, color, pattern, repetition, radiation, emphasis, and unity found there. Ask the children to bring to class various examples of nature's abundant store of leaves, twigs, seeds, weeds, rocks, fossils, stones, honeycombs, bird nests, nuts, pods, seashells, and pine cones. Encourage the use of these as inspirational subject matter for line drawings and paintings.

COLOR AWARENESS

Review color knowledge assimilated in earlier grades. Introduce the children to art projects that demand multiple color choices such as: collage (cut-and-paste) employing colored construction papers, tissue papers, or assorted fabrics; printing with found objects on colored paper; weaving with colored papers; painting imaginative themes with crayon or oil pastel on colored paper; mosaics utilizing colored construction paper, creating a color environment in the classroom combining crepe paper, balloons, hula hoops, colored cellophane, and ribbons.

Self-portraits and portraits of classmates are popular as themes for linoleum prints in the upper grades. It is best to make the preliminary sketch with a blunt felt-nib pen, small brush and ink, or black crayon, which relates more closely to the final product.

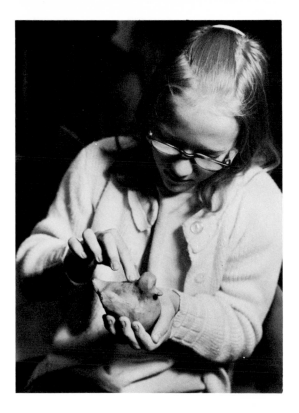

Encourage youngsters to experiment with an expanded range of colors including the tints and shades. Discuss the effects of warm and cool colors in a painting and in an environment. Call attention to the possibilities of related colors—those adjacent to each other on the color wheel. Children at this stage are now often ready to tackle the intricacies of color neutralization, obtained by mixing a color with its complementary hue (opposites on the color wheel) and appreciate the subtle yet effective contrast of subdued colors next to bright intense colors. In watercolor and tempera painting the children can be guided to mix new colors for a particular effect or mood—the earth colors, siennas, umbers, ochres, browns, and grays.

COLLAGE

Build on knowledge gained in the primary grades. Introduce cut-and-paste projects that require the creating of pattern or low-relief effects achieved by folding, fringing, pleating, weaving, and curling the paper. Direct attention now to positive and negative shapes. Suggest how the positive shape obtained by cutting a shape out of a sheet of paper and the negative shape (the piece left over after cutting) can be effectively employed and juxtaposed in a collage design. Introduce colored tissue paper, either torn or cut, as a collage element. Encourage color discoveries by suggesting the youngsters build several tissue layers beginning with the lightest colors first, using white construction paper as the background and liquid laundry starch as the adhesive. Encourage the

Encourage children to hold the clay in their hands when modeling three-dimensional forms, especially in the beginning stages. Youngsters can manage fairly successful pinch pots if the technique is explained and demonstrated.

use of tissue paper collage designs for notebook covers, canister covers, or placemats.

Collage projects lend themselves beautifully to abstract or nonobjective designs inspired by sounds: a whisper, shout, click, swish, hum, rattle, squeak, roar, or thunderclap.

PRINTMAKING

The vegetable clay stamp and found object prints introduced in the primary grades can now be augmented with oil pastel colors as a final embellishment. At this stage the youngsters can successfully manage the *collograph* or *cardboard relief print*. (See the section "Collographs" in Chapter 8.) A variety of prints involving linear interpretations are possible at this age level. Recommended techniques include: the *glue line print* (see the section "Glue Line Prints" in Chapter 8); the string print, a process in which string is glued to a cardboard plate in a free design, allowed to dry, then inked and printed; the *polystyrene sheet (meat tray) print* in which lines are indented into the tray with a pencil, the tray then inked with a roller and printed, the indented lines appearing white in the final print; *the monoprint (single print)* in which a sheet of glass (its edges taped) or a rectangle of light-colored formica is inked with a roller. Oil ink in black or dark colors is recommended. A basically linear composition is made by scratching through the ink with a pencil, Q-tip, edge of cardboard, or other tool. A sheet of newsprint or tissue is placed over the inked surface and the monoprint is pulled. Use turpentine to clean inked surface and ink roller. It is recommended that a table be set aside for monoprinting and

The directness of clay manipulation holds a fascination for children that is universal. This delightful clay figure has a mobility only the clay medium captures so well. Youngsters can make a figure in clay perform many feats—it can walk, sit, twist, dance, bend, even stand on its head, as illustrated in the clay creature on the following page.

the number of students printing be limited to four at a time. Be sure to cover the table with newspapers. Children should wear old shirts to protect their clothing.

CERAMICS

At this stage review knowledge the children have gained in earlier school years about clay—its plasticity, possibilities, and limitations. An exploratory session in clay manipulation is again recommended. Previous learnings about the properties of clay should be recapitulated as the children work. They will probably remember that hard clay is difficult to manipulate; that clay, too moist, sags if the supports are not sturdy enough; that appendages break off when clay dries unless they are securely joined to the main structure; that textures and patterns can be made in clay with fingers, pencils and assorted found objects; that a very large solid lump of clay may explode in the kiln unless a provision is made for the air inside to escape. In making large clay animals such as dinosaurs the post and lintel process is often recommended. (See the section "Clay" in Chapter 8.) This basic structure can then be modeled, added to, condensed, or stretched until the youngsters achieve the characteristic body form they desire. Children at this stage can explore more complex techniques in pottery making. The simple pinch pot can become a double-pinch pot container by joining two pinch pots of the same size. Use clay slip to seal the junctions. Cut out openings and add feet and spouts for individualized pots. Instruct the youngsters in clay scoring and slip-cementing processes.

A GROWING ART VOCABULARY

The following words should become part of the youngster's growing art vocabulary in addition to those recommended for the primary grades: background, balsawood, batik, brayer, carbon paper, cellophane, ceramics, collage, collograph, color wheel, complementary colors, composition, cone, contrast, contour line, corrugated cardboard, crafts, cube, cylinder, detail, enamel, foreground, form, found materials, gauge, gum eraser, hue, incised relief, India ink, inking slab, intensity, landscape, linoleum, linoprint, masking tape, Masonite, monoprint, mosaic, negative shape, papier-mâché, plaster, plywood, positive shape, poster, pyramid, radiation, railroad board, rasp, relief, rubber cement, scoring (clay, paper), shade, shellac, sketch, slab of clay, slip (clay), spectrum, stabile, staple, *still life*, stitchery, tie and dye, tint, turpentine, unity, value, variety, wedging (clay).

SUGGESTED SUBJECTS OR THEMES FOR
CHILDREN'S ART PROJECTS AGES SEVEN, EIGHT,
AND NINE: GRADES THREE AND FOUR

Spring Cleaning
Washing the Family Car
Boarding the School Bus
On the School Bus
At the Airport
At the Gas Station
On the Subway
Window Shopping
On the Train
A View from a Plane

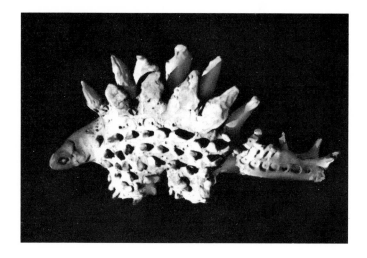

The post and lintel technique of constructing and modeling a dinosaur is illustrated here and later described in detail in the section on Clay. A completed clay dinosaur is also shown. Adaptations were made and embellishments added as the piece progressed.

Rare Birds
Bicycle Race
At the Barbershop
At the Dentist's
Three Ring Circus
Undersea Marine Life Station
Fun at the Beach (Swimming Pool)
Kite Festival
Totem Poles
Soap-Box Derby
A Tree House
A Worm's-Eye View of the Earth
The Fair
A Ride in a Helicopter
Disneyland, Six Flags, Marine World, Frontierland
Space Voyage
Tree of Life
The Insect World
Lines Around You
Fifty Fathoms Deep
Playing a Musical Instrument
A Bouquet of Flowers
Autumn Trees
Sounds Around Us
Prehistoric Animals
Traffic Jam
The Flower Market
Winter Carnival
Waiting in the Rain

The felt-nib pen X-ray drawing on this page is an excellent example of art expanding a child's horizons. The paper was divided into three sections, the top for the structure of the tree above ground, the middle for the tree's roots underground, and the bottom for the various soil and rock strata. Upper grade youngsters drew the trees from life and then sought science books for help with soil beds and root formations.

AGES NINE, TEN, AND ELEVEN: GRADES FIVE AND SIX

DRAWING, DESIGNING, PAINTING

Whenever possible take the youngsters on sketching field trips. Scout and select interesting sites to draw: building constructions, shopping malls, harbors, bridges, gas stations, boat marinas, natural museums, zoos, fire stations, botanical gardens, farm buildings, fairgrounds in operation, airports, and amusement centers. At this stage, children can be guided to create interest and movement in their compositions by varying the placement of the images or motifs within the picture plane. For example, figures, objects, or buildings might begin on different foreground levels and terminate at varying heights in the background. Shapes can be juxtaposed or overlapped to create compositional unity and space-in-depth. Challenge the youngsters to see the possibilities of positive and negative shapes in their pictures. Usually the more varied the objects or positive elements are in size and shape, the more resolved and satisfying the background design becomes.

Continue implementation of expressive drawing approaches utilizing both contour and free-gesture techniques. Children now may attempt to achieve value contrast through shading, stippling, hatching, crosshatching, and washes. They will need help and reassurance in the interpretation of color values and of cast shadows and reflections.

At this stage the maturing youngster will begin to realize the importance of creating avenues into the

The classroom and classmates provide youngsters in school with constant inspiration for drawing subject matter. Compare this contour drawing by an Iowa City fifth grader with the one on page 47 from Osaka, Japan.

composition by incorporating lines and shapes that terminate at the boundaries of the paper. These avenues lead the viewer into the picture and usually the more avenues created, the more opportunities the child has to exploit a variety of colors and values in the resulting shapes.

Unless the youngster specifically requests the teacher's help, it is wiser not to introduce perspective rules or foreshortening techniques at this stage. However some children will want their pictures to "look right" and will more than likely need assistance in making their fences stand straight, sidewalks lie flat, and roads disappear over a distant hill. To help them, remember that fence posts are usually drawn parallel to the sides of the page, division lines in sidewalks are usually drawn at angles to a distant vanishing point, and roads usually diminish in size as they progress in space. Although the youngsters strive for the "right" proportions in their figures the teacher must somehow convince them that drawing something "realistically" right does not always make it "artistically" right. They should be reminded that many noted artists have often ignored all the so-called rules of perspective and proportion to produce works of great impact and beauty.

To expand the children's knowledge and appreciation of master drawings and paintings the teacher should introduce them to the art of Albrecht Durer, Rembrandt Van Rijn, Eugene Delacroix, Katsushika Hokusai, Paul Klee, Edgar Degas, Vincent Van Gogh, Henri Matisse, Pablo Picasso, Ben Shahn, and Willem De Kooning. Call their attention also to the cave drawings found at Altamira and Font du Gaume, the strong and attenuated figures of African and Australian primitives, the sumi-e ink drawings of China and Japan, and the expressive graphics of the American Indian and Eskimo.

COLOR AWARENESS

Review color theories and color discoveries made in previous grades. Recapitulate data concerning primary, secondary, and intermediate colors; the color wheel, complementary and related color schemes; color values, the tints and shades; the means of neutralizing or dulling colors; the psychological effect of colors on people; the colors emphasized in advertising media; the colors of ceremonies, celebrations, customs, and rituals; and the symbolic meanings of colors in different cultures.

Use mood music as a background for free, expressive painting. Whenever possible take the youngsters to exhibits featuring contemporary color and light shows. Encourage the children to construct a color "environment" or "happening" using found materials such as ribbons, wrapping paper, cellophane, yarn, balloons, hula hoops, crepe paper in sheets and streamers, giant paper flowers, fabric samples, and beach towels. Suggest that the youngsters paint the resulting "assemblage" in bold tempera or fluorescent colors.

Continue to build color awareness by directing the attention of the children to color exploitation in their everyday world—to billboards, the new urban murals, magazine covers, packaging, athletic uniforms, "mod" clothing, interior decoration, foods, book jackets, album covers, new cars, store fronts, and shopping malls.

Augment the youngsters' color knowledge and appreciation by scheduling films on color in art and life and by exposing them to fine reproductions (originals, when possible) of paintings by Henri Matisse, Hans Hofmann, Odilon Redon, Amadeo Modigiliani, Pierre Bonnard, Paul Gauguin, Claude Monet, William Turner, and Piet Mondrian. Include contemporary colorists such as Sam Francis, Karel Appel, Mark Rothko, Clifford Still, Jackson Pollock, Stuart Davis, Morris Louis, and Kenneth Noland.

COLLAGE

Recapitulate previous learnings and discoveries in collage including the exploration of positive and negative shapes, creating unity and shallow space through overlapping of shapes, and suggesting partially three-dimensional effects through paper folding, fringing, and curling. Introduce paper scoring to students who are ready for more skillful challenges. Demonstrate the scoring technique: Place paper to be scored on a thick padding of newspapers. Use blunt point of scissors or similar tool and indent the curved line desired into the paper, then carefully fold along the indented line. Be careful not to cut the paper when indenting. Youngsters at this state can master more intricate detail in their paper cutting but they, too, must be guided to complete their large, basic shapes first.

Challenge the students to scout for unusual found objects to use in their collages—wallpaper and rug samples, fabric remnants, discarded building materials. (See Appendix E.) Subject matter themes for collage projects at this level can be more complex and sophisticated.

PRINTMAKING

Although the various printmaking processes introduced in previous grades (the vegetable or found object print, the collograph, the glue line print, and the monoprint) can be repeated at this age level, the maturing youngsters will respond now to more complicated and challenging print techniques. Linoleum printing is a favorite, especially with the boys, because of the opportunity to use the various gouges. More tools, equipment, and time are required for advanced printmaking. Organization of inking, printing, and cleanup stations is a very important requisite. (See the section "Linoleum Prints" in Chapter 8.) Additional sophisticated printmaking processes are possible where special presses are available. These include, among other techniques, engravings utilizing discarded x-ray plates (use laundry bleach to clear), and polystyrene sheets or glossy-coated cardboard pieces as the printing plates.

CERAMICS

Review previously assimilated discoveries about clay and clay manipulation. Provide for a session of clay exploration together with a class discussion of the clay aesthetic, its possibilities and limitations. More complex ceramic modeling may now be attempted. Popular subject matter themes for this age

group are: legendary heros and heroines, Biblical and equestrian figures, animals and their young, portraits and self-portraits, animals in combat, and mother and child depictions. Youngsters now place a strong emphasis on achieving correct proportions, action, and characteristic detail. The teacher must be prepared to offer sympathetic guidance when called upon. In most instances refer the student to the original inspirational source of the subject matter—the figure or the animal itself. If this is not possible, then to a film, color slide, or photograph. Neither overly praise the purely naturalistic approach often

Ancient ceramic Haniwa horse from Japan. Hollow clay cylinders form the basic shape. Note the simplicity and directness and how additional clay coils were flattened to add details.

admired by the child nor harshly criticize it; instead, introduce the youngster to those styles, techniques, and interpretations that are aesthetically more expressive, restrained, and universal. Obtain and exhibit reproductions, either in color or black and white, of ceramic sculpture from ancient cultures—Chinese Tang figurines, Japanese Jomon and Haniwa pieces, and clay vessels in the form of human figures from Mexico and Peru, especially the expressive creations of the Tarascans. In the area of pottery the children can progress from the basic pinch and coil pots of earlier grades to double pinch pots, slab containers, and clay patch techniques.

A GROWING ART VOCABULARY

Build on the art vocabulary recommended and, we hope, acquired in previous grades. Augment it with the following new words: armature, assemblage, burnish, cartoon, charcoal, conté crayon, converging lines, crosshatch, distortion, dowel, encaustic, etching, firebrick, fixative, foreshortening, gesture drawing, glaze, gouge, greenware, grog, horizon line, kneaded eraser, lacquer, leather-hard clay, linear, mass, medium, mixed media, mold, monochromatic, montage, motif, neutralization of color, ochre, opaque, palette, paraffin, patina, perspective, poster board, printing press, proportion, raffia, reed, related colors, repoussé, sepia sienna, Sloyd knife, solder, symbol, symmetry, technique, terra cotta, tessera, transfer paper, translucent, transparent, umber, vanishing point, vermiculite, wedging board, woodblock, X-acto knife.

SUGGESTED SUBJECTS OR THEMES FOR
CHILDREN'S ART PROJECTS AGES TEN, ELEVEN,
AND TWELVE: GRADES FIVE AND SIX

Great Moments in Sports
Hot Rod Races
Space Platforms
Deep Sea Divers
Cities in Outer Space
Self-Portraits
Portraits of Classmates
Thanksgiving Celebration
Landscapes
Cityscapes
Nature Studies
Machines and Motors
Dune Buggies
Horse Show
Block Party
4-H Fair
Amusement Park
The Shopping Mall
The Rodeo
Things on a Table (Still Life)
Track Meet
Animals in Their Habitats
A Bird's Eye View of the Earth
People in Costume or Uniform
Athletes in Action
The Marching Band
Garage Sale
Dream Cars and Boats
Musical Instruments
String Quartet
Dancers of the World
Design in Nature: Radiation

Animals: Endangered Species
Legendary Figures
Warriors in Armor
Fashion Show
Motorcycles
County Fair, State Fair
Flying Trapeze Act
Picnic Lunch
Log Rolling
Air Show

METAL REPOUSSÉ

Metal embossing or tooling is an art project upper grade children enjoy. The teacher should provide a number of stimulating visual resources for motivation so the youngsters can create their own designs. Discourage the use of molds or stereotyped patterns. Preliminary drawings may be made on newsprint, manila paper, or notebook sheets. Size should be limited to perhaps 6″ × 9″ or 9″ × 9″ for best results. The illustrations of copper repousse at left and on facing page are 9″ × 12″. Fish, insects, birds, and jungle animal themes provide excellent textural exploitation possibilities. Heavy duty aluminum foil or commercially available metal sheeting (36 gauge) is recommended. Tape preliminary drawing to metal sheet as a guide to initial embossing. Use a generous amount of newspaper padding under the metal sheet during the tooling or embossing. To make the relief indentations use a large blunt-point pencil, a ball-point pen, the end of a small water color brush, or commercially available embossing tools. After the basic preliminary line is embossed, remove sketch and work directly on metal sheet. When the design is completely embossed it may be embellished further by applying black shoe polish and wiping it off the raised surfaces. If the budget allows, you can order copper sheeting, emboss it, and give it a beautiful patina employing liver of sulfur coating. Mount metal repousse projects on wood panels for an attractive display.

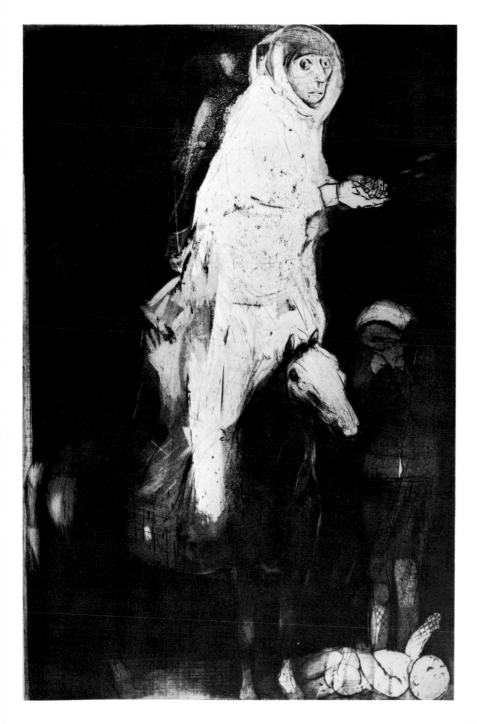

7

AVENUES TO ART APPRECIATION

Children today have infinitely more opportunities to see and appreciate art than ever before. Our burgeoning museums and art centers have open doors, mobile art exhibits tour many cities and states, and giant murals now enliven countless urban walls. Magazines continually and consistently feature articles on art. Colorfully illustrated books on art are published in greater numbers today than ever before, and reproductions of art are available at fairly reasonable prices.

School textbooks in music, social studies, and literature are filled with colorful, correlative art visuals. Art Councils in a number of states promote art festivals and exhibits.

Despite all these opportunities to experience and appreciate art, many school children have minimal exposure to the fine arts. What can classroom teachers or art teacher do to remedy this situation and enrich the lives of their students through art?

One immediate avenue is the correlation of art appreciation with the *doing* of art. To ensure success in this strategy, the teacher will need to requisition color reproductions, color filmstrips, or color slides of

"Espana." Color intaglio. Mauricio Lasansky, 1956, 32" × 21". Collection of the author.

paintings, sculpture, crafts, and architecture. Resourceful teachers have collected and built extensive picture files of their own.

The following list of art projects and suggested correlative reproductions or color slides will provide the teacher with a variety of starting clues for art appreciation lessons.

SUGGESTED
ART PROJECT

Painting: Helping at Home

CORRELATIVE
ART APPRECIATION

Genré paintings of Jan Vermeer, Pieter De Hooch, Andrew Wyeth, Jean Chardin, Grandma Moses, Grant Wood.

Left: *Olmec, Mexico. 1000* B.C. *The Museum of Primitive Art, New York City. Serpentine, Height 4½″;* Center: *"Ashura," Buddhist deity. 8th Century, dry lacquer. Kofuku-ji Temple,*

Nara, Japan. Right: *"The Calfbearer." Greek ca. 560* B.C., *stone, height 70″. A universality of art spirit imbues these sculptures worlds apart!*

Clay Figure Modeling	Clay figures of Greek Tanagra Period, Chinese Tang Period, Japanese Jomon and Haniwa Periods, Peruvian and Guatemalan Primitive Cultures.
Painting: Figure Compositions	Edgar Degas, Paul Gauguin, Pablo Picasso, Francisco Goya, Rembrandt Van Rijn, Thomas Hart Benton, Joseph Hirsch, Ben Shahn, Jacob Lawrence, Robert Gwathmey, George Bellows, Romare Bearden, Max Beckmann, Henri Matisse.
Painting: Self-Portraits	Self-portraits by Vincent Van Gogh, Rembrandt Van Rijn, Pablo Picasso, Paul Gauguin, Albrecht Durer, Max Beckmann.
Painting: Objects on a Table	Still lifes by Paul Cezanne, Odilon Redon, Georges Braque, Pablo Picasso, Jean Chardin, Juan Gris, Andrew Wyeth, William Harnett, Yasuo Kuniyoshi, Bernard Buffet.
Three-dimensional Construction	Sculpture by Alexander Calder, David Smith, Jean Arp, Barbara Hepworth, Louise Nevelson, Pablo Picasso, Henry Moore, Isamu Noguchi, Jean Tingely, Marisol.

Top: *"Self-Portrait." Vincent Van Gogh, 1888, 25½" × 20", Rijkmuseum, Amsterdam. Bottom: "Self-Portrait." Paul Gauguin, 1891, 25⅝" × 18". Metropolitan Museum of Art, New York City.*

Sculpture in Plaster Block	Sculpture of ancient Egypt, Easter Island, Aztec and Mayan cultures, Indian totems.
Mask Making	Masks of North Pacific Indians, Melanesians, Africans, Japanese and Greek Drama and Comedy Masks.
Drawing: Animals	Drawings by Jean Louise Gericault, Rembrandt Van Rijn, Albrecht Durer, Henri Rousseau, Leonardo Da Vinci, and John James Audubon. Indian, Chinese and Japanese animal drawings.
Drawing: Landscape or Cityscape	Paintings by Maurice Utrillo, Maurice Vlaminck, J. M. W. Turner, John Constable, Paul Gauguin, Vincent Van Gogh, Raoul Dufy, Stuart Davis, Bernard Buffet, Dong Kingman, Edward Hopper, Grant Wood.
Printmaking	Prints by Albrecht Durer, Rembrandt Van Rijn, Leonard Baskin, Mauricio Lasansky, William Hayter, Warren Colescott, Gabor Peterdi, Ando Hiroshige, Katsushika Hokusai, Kitagawa Utamaro.

Catalogues of color slides and color reproductions are available from the distributors listed in Appendix D.

Top: "White Vase with Flowers." Odilon Redon, 1916, Museum of Modern Art, New York City. Bottom: "Sunflowers." Vincent Van Gogh, Rijkmuseum, Amsterdam.

8

A PROGRAM IN ACTION

A host of projects and techniques in two and three dimensions recommended for a qualitative elementary art program are described in detail on the following pages. These presentations should prove most helpful to classroom teachers who are quite often unskilled in the basic art processes of painting, printmaking, collage, sculpture, and crafts. Elementary school teachers generally know a great deal about the children in their classes, their characteristics, and their behavior but too often their knowledge of the motivational strategies and the evaluative procedures they must employ to help the child in art is not their strongest area of competence.

The following descriptions of art projects in action encompass both the practical and idealistic teaching aspects. They document motivational possibilities, clarify complex techniques, offer solutions for organizational and supply problems, and suggest applications of reasonable, attainable art criteria.

In no instance is the implication intended, nor is the reader to assume, that the projects and techniques described here are the only viable possibilities; however, they have been tested and found highly successful in situations typical of today's crowded elementary schools, in classrooms filled with eager, bright, dreamy, fidgety, sleepy, tired, energetic, noisy, apathetic, boisterous, talkative, and wonderful children. The colorful illustrations of the children's creative efforts speak for themselves.

A dynamic developmental art program in elementary school should provide children with a variety of in-depth art experiences. Youngsters who sometimes have difficulty achieving success in one technique may blossom in another. The illustra- *tions on facing page, showing children absorbingly engaged in their art endeavors, suggest only a fraction of the creative projects that a qualitative art curriculum includes.*

DRAWING THE FIGURE

What skills and techniques in figure drawing should be introduced and developed in the elementary art program? What can teachers really say to the child about the delineation of the figure? When, if ever, should relative proportions of the human figure be emphasized? These are a few of the critical questions involving figure drawing that confront the elementary classroom teacher. Unfortunately, the strategy most often proposed is "Let the children alone. They will find their own way." This injunction no doubt provides the classroom teacher with a face-saving excuse if the results are less than satisfactory; however, this is hardly the advice given to teachers regarding other basic subject areas, such as math or language.

If teachers want youngsters to grow in their representation of the figure then they must provide learning experiences and practice sessions for such growth.

Illustrations on this and facing page show the honesty of portrayal and the attention paid to characteristic detail when children draw directly from the model.

Fortunately there are some avenues a teacher can pursue to help children develop confidence in figure drawing. They can become more aware of the human figure and its characteristics by employing the posed model in class at every grade level. The delineation of the figure in even the youngest child's drawings does not emerge out of a vacuum. What is wrong then with the close attention, immediate perception, and identification with the figure that the model offers?

Before the students actually begin drawing, a warmup session is recommended. Motivating or leading questions should be asked: What is the model doing? What part of the model do you see from where you are? What is the model wearing? How big is the model's head in comparison to the body? How big are the hands? Put your own hand over your face. Did you realize your hands were so big? How big are your feet? They must be large enough to keep you steady as you walk. Where is the arm the largest? At the shoulder or at the wrist? Where is the leg the largest? At the ankle or near the hips? Where does the body, the leg, or the arm bend? How wide can the feet stretch apart? How high can the arm reach above the head? How far can the body swing around?

As the children draw, guide them to look at the model carefully, to get their eyes full. Caution them against rushing, scribbling, or making hasty, lazy, random lines. Tell them to always look first, then draw. Remind them to make the figure as large as possible, to fill the page with it, so that their classmates can see it from across the room. Sometimes it is helpful if they begin their drawing of a figure starting with the head at the top of the page, unless, of course,

the figure is holding something above his head.

Figure drawing, as all drawing from life, teaches the child to be observant in many ways. It is amazing how quickly the growing, discerning child notices embellishing details such as belts, ribbons, shoelaces, buttons, necklaces, bracelets, pockets, insignia, ruffles, zippers, pleats, glasses, belts, or the pattern of clothes, such as stripes, dots, diamonds, and plaids, using them to enrich his interpretation.

Figure drawing from the model, especially in the upper grades, can often lead to utilization of the figure or group of figures in a painting, collage, print, or mural.

The drawings themselves, either in pencil, pen, or crayon, have a validity and charm of their own. Subject matter themes such as *I am playing ball, I am riding my bike, I am holding my pet, I am skipping rope, I am playing a guitar* lend themselves effectively to space-filling compositions.

In projects where figure drawing is involved, many classroom teachers feel they lack the necessary expertise to guide the youngsters with confidence. They often settle, therefore, for what the children can accomplish on their own without any guidance whatsoever. But what about the child himself? Shouldn't he receive as much help in this activity as he gets in music or science? The wrong kind of direction, however, is not the answer, either. Stereotyped formulas such as stick figures, body and face proportions measured by inches and rulers, and other conforming or restrictive devices should be avoided at all costs.

Motivation for drawing and painting is always more effective when youngsters identify with the subject portrayed. Upper grade students employed pencil, crayon, oil, pastel, and watercolors to create these compositions. Introduce them to the multifigure paintings of Picasso, Gauguin, Toulouse-Lautrec, Degas, Seurat, Bearden, and Jacob Lawrence.

These contour drawings from life are by Japanese grade school children. Observe the careful and explicit delineation of the wrinkles in clothing, the details in shoes and socks, the hair and fingernails.

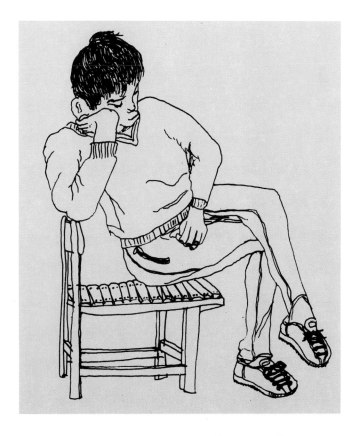

Figure drawing strategies to employ with very young children have been suggested earlier. Tested and proven approaches in figure delineation to whet and hold the interest of the upper-grade youngster follow:

Pose a student model in a colorful costume or sports uniform.

Pose the model in the center of a circle of sketching students so each child sees a slightly different view. Change the action and direction of the model on the next pose.

Introduce new drawing and sketching tools such as the free-flowing felt- or nylon-nibbed markers, ball-point pens, sticks, and India ink.

Pose the student model against a sheet of cardboard or plywood approximately 4 × 8 feet, in any case slightly larger than the model. This will help the youngsters relate the posed figure to the boundaries of their paper. Cover the board with drapery for a more exciting background.

Demonstrate new approaches in drawing the figure: contour, gesture, scribble, mass. In contour line drawing the student is instructed to look intently at the model as he draws and to refer to his sketch or paper only at critical junctures.

Suggest a pose with more than one student taking part. Stage the model in conjunction with a still-life arrangement.

Challenge the students to use their imaginations in drawing. Let the action or stance of the figure trigger a theme or idea for them.

Have different models take 5-minute turns in posing such as playing ball, cheerleading, and dancing, and

The figure lends itself beautifully to a variety of interpretations. Top: A child drew herself with her pets and, of course, the radiating sun! Bottom: An oil pastel painting inspired by a classmate's pose. The teacher helped by providing the trappings that transformed the model into an exciting and colorful subject.

recommend that students overlap the figures as they draw.

Vary the size of the paper the children use for sketching. Try a 9 × 18 inch or 12 × 24 inch sheet for a standing figure.

If you have sufficient space in your classroom, give the youngsters the opportunity to work on large 24 × 36 inch paper with large brushes, wide-nib felt markers, or large chunk crayons.

Introduce a variety of papers to draw on: plain newsprint, cream or gray manila, white drawing, assorted colored construction, wallpaper samples, brown wrapping bogus, or classified ad pages from the daily news.

Let the youngsters try the cut or torn paper technique in their interpretation of the figure. In this method they refer to the model and cut or tear the shapes directly without any preliminary drawing.

Older children might benefit from the use of resource material, such as a real skeleton, providing the opportunity for a study of bone structure and junctures.

Inexpensive, lightweight 18 × 24 inch drawing boards can be constructed out of heavy-weight chipboard, cardboard, or standard Upsonboard. The edges of these boards can be protected with overlapping masking tape. During the drawing session these boards can be tilted against the table or desk giving the child a better working position from which to view the model.

For action or gesture drawing which requires a free approach, the children should be encouraged to hold the crayon, pencil, or chalk horizontally as they sketch rather than upright as in writing.

Illustrated on the following two pages are progress figure drawings in black crayon on 12" × 18" paper. Theme: "Brushing My Teeth" or "Combing My Hair." Approximate drawing time: 50 minutes. Note how early base line moves up in later years to become room baseboard; how the face in the mirror appears in upper grade drawings.

James, age six.

Jimmy, age seven.

Jeff, age nine.

Linda Kay, age six.

Janice, age eight.

Jane, age eight.

Loren, age ten.

John, age ten.

Rory, age eleven.

Halli, age nine.

Kathy, age ten.

Kathy, age eleven.

Promote self-identification through figure drawing experiences that have meaning for the youngsters: playing a musical instrument, riding a bike or motorcycle, performing a dance, cheerleading, roller skating, playing football, basketball, baseball, volleyball, tennis, standing under an umbrella in the rain, balancing on a fence or rail, skipping rope, holding a pet, flying a kite, tumbling, twirling a baton, twisting a hula hoop, diving into a pool, jumping on a trampoline, casting for fish, romping with a dog.

Fifth and sixth grade youngsters painted these sophisticated self-portraits on black construction paper using oil pastels in an impressionistic style. Note the perceptive and sensitive treatment of the eyes, eyelids, and planes of the face. The birds add an effective counterpoint. Iowa City, Iowa. Facing page: These line drawings are on 12" × 24" paper.

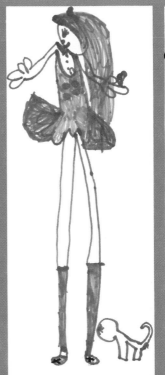

Drawing landscapes or cityscapes on the site is recommended but some situations make it inadvisable. Illustrations center and bottom on facing page as well as oil pastel above show what can develop when upper grade youngsters draw from selected color slides projected on a screen. First the teacher showed towers, steeples, etc., which were drawn in the top one-third of the page, then facades, store fronts, etc. were projected for the middle plane and finally street furniture, trucks, cars, etc. to complete the foreground.

DRAWING THE LANDSCAPE

While very young children in the primary grades enjoy drawing simple themes and single objects such as a house, butterfly, car, tree, or animal, maturing youngsters often respond to the challenge of the complex composition, the landscape and the city-scape. They are now more interested in outdoor sketching and the excitement of field trips. The busy and infinitely varied world beckons and unfolds at their doorsteps:

The building construction down the street
The challenging perspective down an alley
The colorful and crowded shopping center
The big city skyscrapers
The county fair
The cluster of farm houses on a country road
The city park bandstand
The courthouse square
The service station
The bus, train, and airport terminals
The boat marina
The school building and yard
The harbor with its ships
The factories and foundries
The view from a classroom or bedroom window
The amusement park
Special places such as Disneyland, Six Flags, Frontier-
   land.

These sites can become the inspiration for their sketches, compositions, and paintings. A variety of media can be used for outdoor sketching: pencil,

This page. Center: *Preliminary drawing in permanent black ink and bold felt point pen.* Bottom: *Oil pastels, applied richly but not covering ink lines.*

charcoal, ball-point pen, felt-nib marker, stick and ink, chalk, and crayon.

Many youngsters on sketching field trips draw with confidence, but a number will often besiege their teachers with such perplexing questions as: "What should I draw first?" "Where should I start on the page?" "Should I put everything I see in my picture?"

Sometimes the complex view overwhelms them. Sometimes the spatial and perspective problems confuse them. Fortunately there are proven avenues to landscape and cityscape drawing that teachers have found worthwhile in guiding children. In one approach, the teacher recommends that the child begin with a very light pencil or chalk sketch to establish the basic shapes. Once the youngster has established his general outline, he can develop details and value.

Another strategy that is quite successful, especially when the view is complex, is to suggest that the children begin drawing the shape in the center of the site—a doorway, perhaps, a telephone pole, window, tree, silo, small section of a building—draw it as completely as they can, then proceed to draw the shape above it and below it, to the right and left of it, and so on until they fill the page to the borders of their paper. They will find that incomplete shapes touching the paper's edges will form avenues into their compositions. Then guide them to continue their drawing, adding details, patterns, textures, and shadows as they desire.

Problems youngsters have with defining distance in space often can be clarified by an understanding of the following guidelines: Objects or shapes in foreground, or closer to the observer, are usually drawn larger and lower on the page. Objects farther away from the observer, or in the background, are usually drawn smaller and higher on the page. An effective space is created by overlapping components or shapes, such as a fence or tree against a building.

Simple perspective principles, based on the use of the horizon line, vanishing points, and converging lines, should be introduced only when the youngster indicates a need for them.

Sketching field trips should be undertaken only with adequate planning and preparation on the part of both teacher and students. If possible, exciting subject matter should be scouted by the teacher beforehand. Avoid the barren view or the monotonous vista that provides little opportunity for contrasting and varied space breakup.

A class discussion prior to the field trip or sketching excursion is a means of emphasizing specific challenges in advance. Things to look for might include: the architecturally significant characteristics of the buildings, problems to be solved in drawing things further away, value contrasts of dark window panes in daylight, foreground space to be allowed for steps and porches, suggestions for making fences recede, walls stand straight and sidewalks lie flat, and varied solutions for effective handling of foreground and background space.

The teacher should remind the students that in drawing the landscape or cityscape they may use the artist's creative prerogatives of changing, adding, deleting, or simplifying what they see at the site. The criterion is not necessarily photographic reality or measured perspective. If the students wish, they may add more trees, telephone poles, air vents or windows; they may change a roof line or the cast of a shadow; they may ignore and delete a parked car or a poster on a wall. Each decision they make, however, should be qualified by design considerations so that the final composition embodies unity through effective juxtaposition of elements, repetition of shapes, sensitively observed details, directional lines, overlapping of forms, textural interests, a variety of positive and negative areas and spaces, and an exciting balance of dark and light values.

Top: *"Holiday Spirit." Oriental landscape. Lamar Dodd, 1959, 30″ × 42″;* Center: *English landscape, Ted Ramsay, 1970, 16″ × 20″;* Bottom: *American landscape, Frank Wachowiak, 1952, 24″ × 36″.*

Youngsters look at everyday objects with new understanding when they draw them seriously and perceptively. Widen their horizons by introducing them to exciting artifacts and antiques as subject matter for art expression. A coffee grinder, railroad lantern, kerosene lamp, egg beater, mantle clock, farm tools, musical instruments, and ancient sewing machines take on new dimensions through sensitive drawing. Discover your own Americana treasures, then share them with your students through art!

DRAWING THE STILL LIFE

The still-life arrangement, whether as inspiration for drawing, painting, print or collage, is an especially effective means of encouraging keen observation and awareness, developing a sensitive perception of shapes and proportions, appreciating the subtle space achieved through overlapping of objects, and providing the added bonus of initiating a growing interest in and *appreciation of common, everyday things.* Children from the first grade on can be encouraged to discover hidden beauty and aspects of design and form in the ordinary bottles, teapots, lanterns, clocks, musical instruments, kitchen utensils, and potted plants that comprise the typical still life.

From the third or fourth grade on, youngsters can be guided to see the limitless design possibilities in still-life compositions. The best still-life arrangements are similar in many respects to complex cityscapes— for example, a tableau of buildings may echo a cluster of bottles and present the same compositional challenges.

In selecting objects for a still-life arrangement, teachers and students should scout a variety of found objects: small, short, tall, simple, complex, organic, textured, and plain. Antique shops, secondhand stores, basements, garages, army surplus warehouses, rummage sales, flea markets, and attics can provide rich sources for unusual and visually stimulating objects that can contribute to exciting still lifes. Eschew the trite, the miniature figurine, or vase.

The still life in various forms is always around us. We live in a world of still-life arrangements: the piled-up desk, the cluttered kitchen sink, the open garage, cupboard or closet, the box of playground equipment, the table set for a meal.

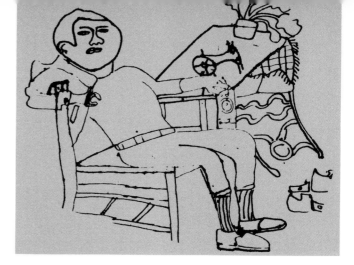

The placement of the various objects in a still life is critical to the ultimate success of the composition or design. Arrange them, for example, on an antique table, old sewing machine, rocker, chair, a step ladder, window ledge, desk top, or on the floor in the middle of the classroom where the children can be seated in a circle as they draw. Utilize a variety of heights or levels (use cardboard cartons or wooden crates as supports); plan overlapping items and an informal or asymmetrical balance. Use assorted fabrics, colorful beach towels, fish nets, bedspreads, quilts, or tablecloths as drapery to unify the separate elements or to suggest movement from one object to another. For best results, it is recommended that all students be afforded a clear and fairly close view of the still-life arrangement.

In most instances, the more objects that are used in a still-life grouping, provided, of course, that they are arranged at different levels and with varied negative and positive shape exploitation, the more opportunities the youngsters have for selection and rejection. In the same vein, the more objects the children utilize in their compositions, the more effectively, and richly

On occasion, the teacher, with the students, will arrange a still-life set-up. In this project, youngsters combined magazine ad cutouts and oil pastel. Realism should not be the criterion. Children will choose colors and patterns they like. Notice, left, how one child captured in his own way the shapes of the owl, lamp, mask, and clock.

they fill the pictorial space and build their designs.

There is no one way for youngsters to begin drawing the still life, as veteran teachers have discovered. One strategy, however, that children respond to, and have success with, is the following: Have them begin by drawing the central object in the still life from their point of view and placing it in the middle of their paper. They then continue drawing the next object to it, above it, below it, left and right of it, and so on, until they have filled the page. This means, of course, that the more varied and complex the still life itself, the more space-filling the drawing will be.

Another tactic is to have the students select items from a general store of still-life material, choosing one object at a time to sketch at their desks, building their compositions gradually, employing the principles of variety, overlapping, repetition, and informal balance.

Some teachers recommend to their students that they make a light, tentative sketch in pencil, charcoal, or brush and ink to obtain a general, allover composition. This preliminary drawing is then developed, stage by stage, utilizing value (light and dark) effects, pattern, texture, shading, and linear emphasis.

The most ordinary, everyday item is worthy of drawing, but artists have often found that objects which relate to or fit the human form have a special life quality, a natural contour that lends itself to effective drawing. For example: shoes, gloves, hats, caps, jackets, even a body-hugging rocking chair! The beautiful drawings on this page are by upper grade youngsters from Athens, Georgia and Evanston, Illinois.

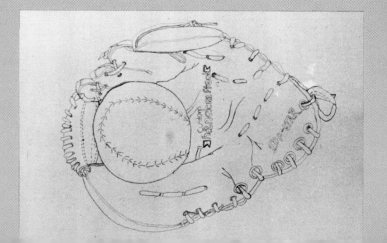

The still-life interpretations on this and facing page are testimony to the variety of approaches children can choose in making their expressive statements. Left to right: Crayon, grade 1; tissue collage, grade 3; watercolor, grade 4; found materials collage, grade 5; and oil pastel, grade 6. All exhibit a successful exploitation of the picture plane.

Youngster completing the painting of a rhinoceros he contributed to a group mural with a jungle theme. The preliminary sketches were made with brush and black tempera. The murals are on exhibit in the children's ward of a community hospital in Athens, Georgia.

DRAWING ANIMALS

Most children respond enthusiastically to drawing experiences where pets and other animals are the subject in question. Girls at the upper elementary school level are especially interested in drawing horses. However, if the drawing of animals is to be a rewarding and valid experience for these youngsters, opportunities for observing a variety of live animals must be provided whenever possible.

The teacher can help by arranging field trips to zoos, aquariums, and natural museums. Equally exciting opportunities to observe animals in action or repose can be found at horse and dog shows, circuses, parades, farms, state or county fairs, animal shelters, or national parks. Pets brought to class provide still another exciting and immediate source of drawing inspiration.

Pencil, stick and ink, and felt-nib pens are recommended for small-sized sketches. Charcoal, conte, chalk, crayon, oil pastel, and blunt-nib ink markers can be used effectively on large compositions. Drawing surfaces suggested include newsprint, cream or gray manila paper, colored construction paper, brown Kraft or butcher paper, and the classified sections of newspaper. A simple, effective yet inexpensive drawing board can be constructed from the side of a large cardboard carton. Commercially available Upson board ¼ inch thick, cut into rectangles 18 × 24 inches and edged with masking tape, is especially recommended. These boards can also be used as drawing surfaces on the often minisized classroom desks.

The animal world has always proven fascinating to child artists, and the subject matter of the animal kingdom is limitless. Top right: A primary grade youngster captures the essence of the leopard by emphasizing his spots. Center and bottom: More sophisticated oil pastels by upper grade students who sketched from mounted animals at a museum in Iowa City.

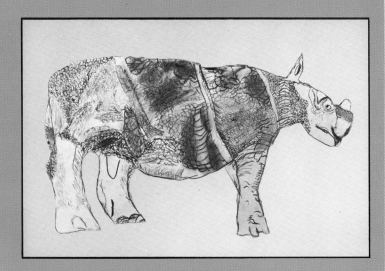

An animal drawing experience might begin with a field trip to a zoo. Prior to the excursion, the teacher and children should discuss the special characteristics of zoo animals including the unique features of the various species—their stance, action, and special physical attributes. Attention might be called, for example, to the textural pattern of the thick-skinned rhino, the wrinkled and leathery face of the orangutan, the repeated yet varied spots of the leopard, the rhythmic rings of the armadillo, the subtle variations of the zebra's stripes, and the gracefully curved horns of the antelope.

When the youngsters begin sketching, they should be encouraged to draw rather generous forms which make the most economical use of the paper's proportions. The larger the drawing, the more opportunities the student has to define and exploit characteristic details, patterns, and textures.

These life drawings might be limited to a delineation of significant details, to an expressive line sketch that might capture the spirit of the animal, rather than to attempt a completed study. Many of the refinements and textural nuances can be added later when the children return to the classroom.

It is recommended that older children on sketching excursions limit their drawing to a single animal, developing the study in depth. This practice is more beneficial than rushed and cursory attempts to draw several different animals in the limited time usually allowed. If scheduling permits, the teacher may plan subsequent visits so that the youngsters will have ample opportunity to sketch a variety of animals. The student might also be encouraged to draw detailed

Elephants and rhinos are favorite jungle animals in children's drawings. They especially enjoy delineating the fantastically textured and bumpy hide of the rhino.

studies of an animal's *eye, ear, tail, hoof, snout,* or *horns.*

Suggest that the students draw their animals in some characteristic action such as eating, resting, climbing, bathing, walking, running, or feeding their young. Older children can be challenged to note the individual stance of an animal: the swinging rhythm of a chimpanzee, the arching stretch of a giraffe, the sway of the elephant's trunk, or the nervous tension of a horse's legs—all serving as clues to the interpretation of the animal's spirit and disposition.

Careful, deliberate observation and sensitive handling of the drawing line are two fundamental requirements in animal drawings. For inspiration suggest that the youngsters look at selected animal drawings: Rembrandt's lion and elephant, Delacroix's horses, as well as those by Chinese Han and Sung artists, Durer's squirrel, hare, and rhinoceros, Wyeth's birds, Sosen's monkeys and Saito's cats.

Drawing or sketching from the animal itself is the primary recommendation, of course, but, when this prospect is out of the question, supplemental motivation, including color slides, films, filmstrips, opaque projections of magazine and book illustrations and photos provided by zoos, educational services, and governmental conservation agencies can provide the necessary vicarious enrichment. In the primary grades, the visual material might be examined and then the illustrations tacked to the bulletin board for further reference. Mounted photographs fulfill a definite need, but it should be made clear to the students that *photos are for inspirational and informational reference only and not for exact copying or tracing.*

Top: *Drawing by Dutch artist Rembrandt von Rijn.* Center: *Drawing inspired by visit to the zoo, Ann Arbor, Michigan.* Bottom: *Woodblock by Kiyoshi Saito, contemporary Japanese artist. Note how the composition fills the space and how the grain of the wood itself is exploited as part of the design.*

The youngsters need to be reminded, also, to consider the entire composition in their animal drawings. In too many instances, the animal is just drawn in the middle of the paper without any reference to the possibilities of interesting background space. To help the students in this respect, the teacher might initiate a discussion on the handling of the surrounding space, including the introduction of additional elements to enrich the composition such as trees, shrubs, hills, streams, marshes, cliffs, clouds, and other animals in either the background or the foreground. Environmental aspects such as these can be employed to enhance the main subject and create dynamic positive-negative contrast in the drawing.

Unusual and interesting plants, dried foliage, rocks, or flowers can serve as reference material for the animal's habitat. Leaves, plants, and rocks from the immediate school vicinity might be drawn giant-size to become escarpments or jungle trees and vines with the pattern of the foliage complementing the textures and shapes of the animals themselves.

Both in the classroom and on supervised field trips the child should be provided with many opportunities to draw directly from nature's sources. Through these perception-building experiences, the youngsters learn to sharpen their visual responses and to increase their visual repertoire. As they draw in linear form those images and phenomena that impress and excite them, they are learning and expressing themselves at the same time—a dual achievement that bolsters their self-worth.

A mounted owl served as the immediate inspiration for this expressively sensitive drawing by an upper grade youngster. Notice the delineation of the fine feather pattern. The leafy background complements the bird in center. Below: Drawing of fish made as a study for a crayon resist. Grade 5.

Challenge the students to notice the unique features of the animal or animals they have chosen to depict, to discover the characteristics that make one animal different from another as well as the aspects that make them alike.

PAINTING WITH TEMPERA

All children should have the opportunity to express their ideas in paint, whether in tempera, poster colors, or watercolors. High quality tempera paints are rich in color, have excellent coverage, and are often packaged in functional, nonbreakable containers. Children who paint with tempera can apply color over color freely to achieve jewel-like effects or repaint areas they are not satisfied with.

Though classroom teachers are aware of the many possibilities for art expression that tempera paint provides, they often do not include it in their art program because of the housekeeping chores involved. It is true that tempera projects require more materials preparation, careful storage, and expeditious cleanup procedures than watercolor or crayon art; these factors, however, should not prevent teachers from discovering how it can enrich the art repertoire of the children in their classes.

In recent years inventive teachers and art consultants have developed many ways to solve the problems of tempera painting where large classes and limited facilities are involved. Some strategies have proven most expeditious and time-saving. Discarded baby-food jars and half-pint wax milk cartons have been successfully used as containers. Cardboard soda bottle containers and discarded glass tumbler carryalls have been commandeered as carrying cases. The half-pint milk carton can be resealed with clothes-pins or giant paper clips thus preventing the paint from drying between sessions.

New strategies in the preparation, use, and storage of tempera paint have extended its use in elementary schools. Discarded half-pint milk carton fastened with paper clips or clothespins help keep paint moist from one session to another. Giant plastic bags also keep paint in tins from drying out in storage. Facing page: A primary grade child used colorful tempera to depict "A Bunny Rabbit Easter Party." Background is colored construction paper.

Children can help in the preparation of tempera paint, mixing the various hues, tints, and shades and filling the individual paint containers to two-thirds capacity. For a class of 30 children about 60 containers of varying colors should be prepared. At least six white and four black paint containers should be available. All paints should be placed on a table or cart accessible from all sides and low enough so that the various colors are visible. There should be a fairly large watercolor brush for each color or container. Children take turns to choose the initial color they wish and a brush to paint with. When they are through with a color, they return the container with the brush in it to the supply table or cart. This procedure saves valuable time that is so often dissipated in cleaning brushes during the painting session. It is recommended that the children use one color container at a time. In certain situations they may share their colors at their table.

Adequate time should be allotted for cleanup procedures. Brushes, especially the kind with plastic handles and nonrusting ferrules, can be taken out of the paint containers (carefully squeeze or wipe off excess paint in the process) and placed in a large dishpan of soapy water to soak overnight. The next morning they can be rinsed and stored bristle-side up. Unless the paint in the baby food jars can be covered, the paint containers should be stored in an air-tight cupboard or drawer. Investigate the possibilities of placing the individual containers in a tray and sealing the tray in a giant-size plastic bag. Lips and edges of containers should be wiped clean with a damp cloth from time to time. Teachers have discovered that the

A large paper surface gives a child a real opportunity to express ideas in paint. The bold portraits on this and facing page by primary grade youngsters are on 24″ × 36″ heavy manila. Newspapers were placed on the floor and the youngsters painted away! You can also use wallpaper samples as a painting surface.

excess paint does not build up as rapidly if a little liquid paraffin is applied to the container's lip.

Semimoist cakes of opaque paint are now available in tubs or tins from several art supply sources and teachers who have used them recommend them mainly because of their time-saving cleanup and storage factors.

In the primary grades tempera painting is a natural for children. They take to it like ducks to water. The very young child especially enjoys making bold designs in paint and needs only an invitation and the materials to get started. Themes such as *Explosion in a Paint Factory*, *Fourth of July Fireworks*, *Butterflies in a Flower Garden*, *A Make Believe City of the Future*, and *Planets in Outer Space* fire the youngster's imagination and his brush. Colored construction paper provides an excellent surface or ground for tempera paintings because the color of the paper can be exploited as part of the design if necessary. It also helps unify the composition.

Children should be encouraged to make preliminary sketches for their paintings. A line drawing in white chalk or in brush and light colored paint rather than in pencil is recommended. Other background papers for painting include white drawing, cream or gray manila, bogus, oatmeal, chipboard, wallpaper samples, brown wrapping, and classified sections of newspapers.

The following teaching strategies have proved helpful in tempera painting projects:

> Put protective newspapers on the paint supply table and on individual painting areas.

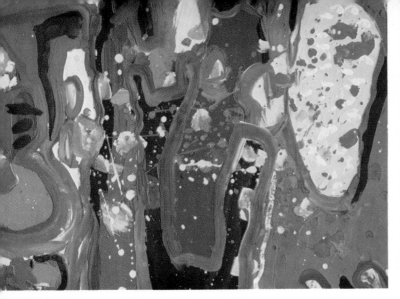

Have a few moist cloths available for accidental paint spills. (Towel remnants are recommended.)

Children can wear old shirts as protective smocks.

Encourage children to repeat colors in various parts of their painting to achieve unity and balance. This minimizes excessive traffic to and from the paint supply table.

Remind children to wipe the excess paint off their brush against the lip of the container.

Caution youngsters to be careful when painting next to a newly painted area if they do not wish colors to run together.

Suggest that children wait until a color is thoroughly dry before painting over it to make a color change.

If brushes must be cleaned during the painting period, remind the students to squeeze out the excess water or the paint in the containers will eventually become diluted.

Storage of paintings should be supervised by the teacher so that wet paintings are not put on top of one another. They may be placed to dry on the floor in the classroom, the hallway, or left on the desks if a recess or lunch period follows the painting class.

In the upper elementary grades children can exploit the varied and complex possibilities of tempera painting because of their developing ability to control the paint and brush. They may design with paint on moist, colored construction paper; utilize the dry-brush and stipple methods to achieve texture and explore the mixed-media processes of tempera and crayon, or tempera and India ink.

Older children can be encouraged to mix a greater variety of tints, shades, or neutralized hues than are already available in the containers. They can use discarded pie tins or aluminum food trays for this

Children enjoy the freedom that tempera paint and large brushes afford. They delight in making nonobjective, abstract, free-form designs, but the teacher can help by suggesting imaginative themes such as "Explosion in a Paint Factory," "Planets in Outer Space," and "Fireworks on the Fourth." Facing page: *Paintings by primary grade children.*

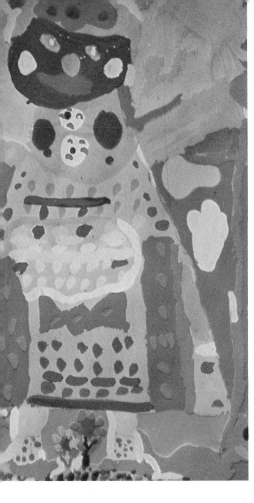

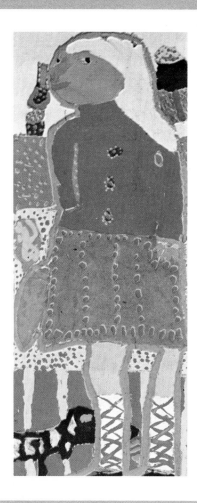

These colorful tempera figure paintings prove once more how truly individual youngsters can be in their art expression even though the materials used are the same and the assigned theme similar; in this case, "A Portrait of My Classmate." Here again the qualitative, in-depth teaching strategies are revealed, the preparation and patience necessary to mix a varied range of tempera hues, the time taken to make a preliminary sketch and to make deliberate, personal choices in applying colors. All the extra effort involved is evident in the final results. Grade 3. Oshkosh, Wisconsin.

purpose. They should be cautioned, however, not to mix more paint than they need. Paint palettes should always be rinsed out at the close of the period.

It is important to remember that growing youngsters cannot rush through a tempera painting project any more than they can hurry through any qualitative endeavor. Sufficient time should be allotted for all phases of the project: preliminary sketching, making deliberate and sensitive color choices, developing contrast, pattern, and detail, evaluating the final stages of the work, and exhibiting the completed paintings.

Tempera painting should be included, if possible, in every elementary art program because it expands and enriches the child's world of color and color relationships.

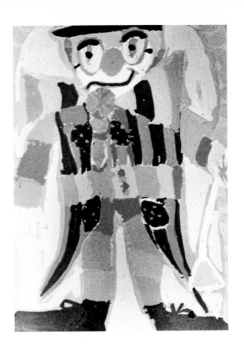

Clowns and imaginative, fantastic creatures have great appeal as painting subject matter for youngsters of all ages.

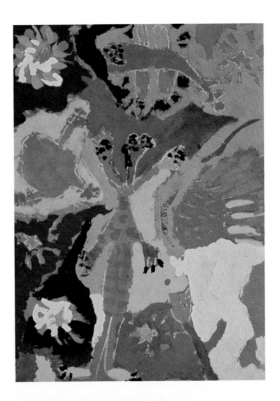

TEMPERA-INDIA INK BATIK

For upper elementary children who have had many experiences in tempera painting, the tempera batik, a resist process which combines liquid tempera painting and India ink overpainting is a unique and challenging mode of artistic expression. The project, however, requires an above-average materials budget and a generous time allotment for the various steps of the process. A good quality liquid tempera, rather than powder or cake, is recommended for this technique. The tempera should be of a creamy consistency; if too thin, the final black ink coating will permeate it to neutralize the colors. Light, bright colors and hues are often preferable to the dark browns, purples, and blues. Add a little white tempera to the darker colors for best effects.

A sturdy paper should be used for the painting surface since the technique requires a final sponging or rinse-off process. Recommended background papers include a strong cream-colored bogus or construction paper in colors of orange, red-orange, pink, magenta, light blue, and light violet. Do not use thin manila or tagboard as the painting surface.

Make the preliminary sketch in school chalk. Encourage the students to vary the pressure of the chalk lines as they sketch, so it will fluctuate from thick to thin. This will be an important consideration in the second phase, where the ink flows into the chalk lines. As students paint, suggest that they paint up to, but not over, the chalklines. The more varied the chalk lines, or the paper surface remaining between two painted areas, the more successful the

Steps in a tempera batik. Top: *Preliminary drawing in school chalk on construction paper. Paint applied up to chalk lines but not over them. Allow to dry completely.* Bottom: *Coat of India ink is applied to tempera painting, allowed to dry thoroughly (several hours), and then rinsed off at sink.* Facing page: *Tempera batik by fifth grader. Oshkosh, Wisconsin.*

composition will be. Remind the youngsters not to paint those areas, shapes, or details that they wish to appear black in the completed composition.

Caution the students, too, that a tempera color painted over another dry tempera color will wash off in the final rinsing process; that is why it is so important to plan the colors before painting. Tempera paint patterns applied over *wet* tempera areas are often quite effective.

Encourage the children to be inventive, daring, and different in their use of colors. Guide them to mix many kinds of blue for a sky and greens for grass.

Unpainted spaces may be left between objects and objects and background, in patterned areas between dots or stripes of color, and wherever areas of black are needed for contrasting effects.

For example, the interstices between fern fronds, bird feathers, fish scales, and tree bark left unpainted will permit the black ink coat to flow into these spaces and create an exciting contrast of color against black.

After all the desired colored areas are painted, the work should be stored to dry completely.

When the painting is thoroughly dry and the chalk wiped off with a cloth, a coat of waterproof black India ink is applied. Use a large watercolor brush or soft bristle utility brush and apply the ink generously in random circular strokes. Remember to utilize newspapers to protect the desk while applying the ink coating.

Allow the ink coat to dry thoroughly before the final rinse or wash. The length of the drying period may vary from a few hours to overnight, depending on the humidity and the season. Do not rinse or spray too soon.

Flower gardens, insects, and butterfly motifs lend themselves especially well to the tempera batik technique. Facing page: These delightful tempera batik self-portraits are by first grade children. 24″ × 36″. Iowa City, Iowa.

For the final washing or rinsing process put the painting on a sheet of Masonite or plastic, slightly larger than the painting itself, and wash off the ink using water from a spray attachment or faucet. In mild weather the paintings may be taken outdoors and rinsed off with a water hose. Be sure the paintings are always on a board during the wash because, if handled when wet, they tear very easily

It is best to begin the rinse in the center of the painting and then rinse outwards. Do not direct the water to one spot too long. The paper may disintegrate. Sometimes a moist sponge or a finger rub can be used to bring out the color in an area where the ink sticks too stubbornly.

When the washing and rinsing process is completed (a final clean rinse is important), use paper towels or newspapers to blot the painting and allow to dry thoroughly. When the completed tempera resist is dry it may be given a coat of clear shellac, clear polymer, or liquid wax to enrich the colors and protect the surface.

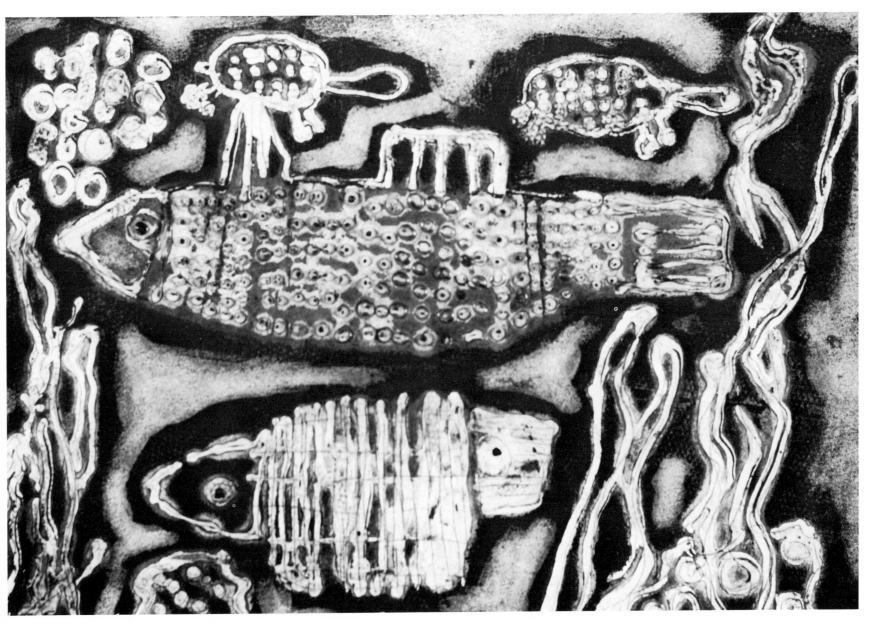

Sometimes the cardboard plate created for a glue line relief print can be inked and mounted as an artifact of singular beauty. Facing page bottom: A "frottage" or rubbing of wood grain proved just the right texture for this cut-out alligator by a young Japanese school child.

Group mural employing the reverse stencil method. Grade 3. Each child cut one animal or bird out of oak tag, pinned it securely to a large 36″ × 48″ colored cardboard (Upsonboard, beaverboard, illustration board) background and applied paint with a spray can. Children who finished their animals first contributed additional trees, flowers, butterflies, snakes. Overlapping of animal shapes created unusual spacial effects. Use lots of newspapers pinned around the cardboard background sheet and on the floor underneath. Spraying should be done in a well-ventilated area or outdoors.

MURALS

If the planning and making of a group mural is to be a valid and worthwhile art experience for the youngsters, the aesthetic requirements of mural art should be considered as carefully as possible. Initially, the students and the teacher must decide whether the project, technique, or subject matter is adaptable to a mural undertaking. Certain themes are more appropriate and stimulating for group mural endeavors because of their complexity or because of their appeal to certain age groups. For very young children the following mural topics are suggested: *A Bird Sanctuary, Land of Make-Believe, Fish in the Sea, Noah's Ark, A Flower Garden, On the Farm, Animals in the Jungle or Zoo, Summer Games.* Older children will respond to the following themes: *Fun at the Beach, Astronauts in Space, Aquanauts on the Ocean Floor, The Rodeo, State Fair, Rock Festival, The Big Parade, From Wheels to Jets: A History of Transportation, Kite Contest, Three-Ring Circus, Playground Fun, Winter Carnival, Block Party, Shopping Mall,* and *Track Meet.*

Before the children begin a mural the teacher might ask the following questions: "What is a mural? Why do artists paint murals? Who made the first murals? Are there any murals in our city, county, or state?" More specifically, the teacher might pose the following queries: "What theme should be used for the mural? What techniques or medium should be employed? How large should the mural be? Where can we work on it? Where could the mural be displayed when completed? How shall each student's contribution to the mural be decided?"

Group mural "Fun on the Playground" painted on a 10′ × 200′ plywood construction barrier. The preliminary linear sketch in black enamel was applied with 1″ wide brushes and helped the youngsters establish their color areas and size relationships. Iowa City, Iowa. Mural now in the collection of the Smithsonian Institute, Washington, D.C.

If, for example, a pin-up (cut-and-paste) mural is decided upon, the following procedure is recommended. When all the youngsters have finished their contributions to the mural and all the individual pieces are tentatively pinned or stapled to the background, the students, with teacher guidance, should devote at least one art session to composing the mural. Here the teacher's tact and gentle persuasion are most important. It should be brought to the attention of the children that a mural is somewhat like a giant painting and consequently requires similar compositional consideration. Look for varied sizes of objects or figures, varied heights, varied breakup of space in foreground and background, overlapping of shapes, avenues leading into the picture, grouping of objects or figures or animals for unity, quiet areas to balance the busy or complex ones, larger figures or objects at bottom, and smaller ones higher up in order to create an illusion of distance or space.

Inevitably, there will be the delicate dilemma where one child's contribution must overlap that of another. Here the teacher can wisely calm troubled waters by pointing out that overlapping shapes create unity and distance suggesting that the children take turns overlapping their figures if they wish. When the separate pieces are finally arranged in a composition that is satisfying, unifying, and colorful, they may be more permanently pinned or stapled down. If the mural is mounted on a separate sheet of Upsonboard, Celotex, or a heavy cardboard, it may be displayed in the school's entrance foyer or in the lunch room for all the children to enjoy.

For example, if *Fun on the Playground* is selected as the subject of the mural, and cut construction paper as the medium, the following questions may have to be resolved: "How many different kinds of games and sports should be included? Let's make a list on the chalkboard. How shall we decide which

game each student will select to portray? How many different areas of the playground will be shown? What pieces of playground equipment should we include? Should all the children on the playground be the same size? Will they all be dressed alike? What patterns might we see in their clothes? What kind of day will it be? Cloudy? Windy? Rainy? What else could you incorporate in your playground mural? What about trees, benches, bushes, goalposts, fences, dogs, birds, drinking fountains, nets, signs?"

Various media and techniques can be employed in making murals. For free, expressive murals that are painted directly on background surfaces such as oaktag, wrapping paper, cardboard, wallpaper or construction paper, use tempera paint, enamels, or latex paints. For murals that are assembled after the children have completed separately assigned parts, use cut colored construction paper, cloth remnants, magazine ads, yarn, chalk, crayon, oil pastel, colored tissue, and found materials.

In the pinup, staple-on type of mural, the children tentatively pin their completed contributions to a selected background. This may be corkboard, Celotex, colored display paper (plain or corrugated) wallboard, burlap, or a large sheet of mattress box cardboard painted appropriately. Children who complete their contributions early may be assigned to do other parts to enhance the composition. Depending on the subject of the mural, these additional embellishments might include trees, flowers, bushes, houses, fences, rocks, butterflies, stars, kites, snowflakes, clouds, rainbows, insects, birds, spiderwebs, planes, sun, moon, rockets, or telephone poles.

The world of nature constantly provides a variety of themes for exciting mural making: animals, fish, and birds. Here the collage or cut colored construction paper technique was employed to create these colorful group murals of animals by primary grade children, birds by intermediate grade youngsters, and fish by upper grade students.

A cat and kittens brought to class by the teacher provided the visual inspiration for this colorful 12″ × 18″ crayon painting by a second grade child. The composition was drawn in line first in a white crayon on orange construction paper. At least three 50-minute class periods were required to complete the crayoning. See page 121 for more interpretations of the same cat and kittens using the same technique.

CRAYON

The wax crayon in assorted colors has been a standard and widely accepted art medium in the elementary schools for over half a century. More recently, resourceful teachers have combined it with other media to provide variety and renewed interest in their art programs. A number of these innovative techniques, including crayon resist, crayon engraving, and multicrayon engraving are described in detail on the following pages.

Unfortunately, the varied and rich potential of the wax crayon with its own singular merits has not always been fully investigated and exploited. The typical classroom projects in crayon are usually weak in color intensity, value contrasts, and textural qual-

ity. Crayon is employed generally as a pallid, sketchy coloring tool instead of the glowing, vibrant, and vitally expressive art medium it can be. It is very important that the rich possibilities of the crayon be identified and explored from the first grade on if children are expected to grow in crayoning skills.

At every grade level, a class session of manipulation and experimentation with the crayons is recommended. Whenever possible, recommend that the youngsters or the school obtain the large 48 or 64 color crayon box with its beautiful range of tints and shades as well as its wide selection of neutralized hues. To help the children achieve the best results, the teacher may have to prompt the youngsters to

The insect world is captured here in these 9″ × 12″ designs by primary grade children utilizing the vibrant, shimmering colors of wax crayon applied richly and boldly over colored construction paper. Two or more class sessions were devoted to this project.

Color slides and photographs of insects were part of the motivation employed. "Press hard!" the teacher encouraged. "Make the crayons sing!"

apply the crayon with a much heavier pressure to bring out the richest colors; employ newspaper padding under their crayoning; point out the excitement of contrasting colors; challenge the youngsters to create patterns of stripes, plaids, strokes, and dots; and stress the utilization of seldom-employed colors such as ochre, umber, sienna, black, gray, and white. Older children can be encouraged to investigate the sensuous applications of crayon over crayon.

The entire mood of a crayon composition changes when color is applied to varicolored or varitextured surfaces. Suggest that the children work on a background other than the commonly used manila or white drawing paper. Explore the effectiveness of colored construction paper as a crayon surface. Student and teacher alike will be surprised and elated by the possibilities of vibrant crayon on pink, red-orange, brown, purple, blue-green, and even black

---

Crayon was used again most effectively in these interpretations of tree houses. Countless motivating questions were asked. What is a tree house? How big must the tree be? How will you climb the tree? What will your tree house look like? Who will

come to visit you? What kind of day will it be? No two tree houses in the class looked alike. One girl even managed to make room for her favorite horse in her tree house!

construction paper. If the children are encouraged to permit areas of the construction paper to show, especially between objects, they will see eventually how the background-paper color can unify their compositions. Suggest that the youngsters try their crayons first on the back of their paper to see how the color of the paper subtly changes the color of the applied crayon.

Preliminary sketches for crayon pictures should be made with a white or very light-colored crayon or white chalk rather than with pencil. This will minimize the frustration children experience when they try to employ a blunt crayon to color the minute details of a pencil sketch.

Encourage the children to use the crayon boldly and expressively. Suggest that colors be repeated to achieve unity. Completed crayon compositions may be given a glowing surface sheen by burnishing or rubbing them with a folded paper towel or facial tissue.

One of the most vexing problems the art teacher faces is that of the children who rush through their crayoning or who quickly color in one or two shapes and claim they are finished. There are no sure-fire remedies for recurring dilemmas such as these but certainly one of the most successful strategies for ensuring a happy, successful outcome in crayon paintings is a teacher's well-planned, resourceful motivation that leads to a richly conceived and detailed preliminary drawing consisting of a variety of shapes which in turn provides the basis for expressive multihued crayoning.

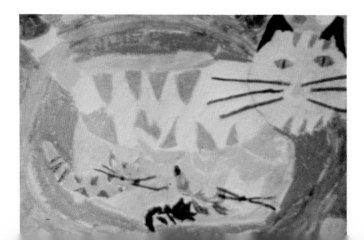

A flower garden comes alive in this beautiful crayon resist painting by a second grade child. Children sometimes call this process "crayon magic." To be successful in this technique the youngsters must be guided to apply the crayons with strong pressure so the wax will resist the watercolor. White drawing or construction paper is recommended for the background. A preliminary drawing in a light color crayon rather than pencil is suggested. Facing page: Underwater themes are most effective for crayon resist paintings. Illustration at top is from a Rangoon, Burma elementary school.

CRAYON RESIST

The combination of the glowing wax crayon and translucent, flowing watercolors on white construction, drawing, or cream manila paper provides an exciting creative experience for children of all ages. Subject matter themes that are rich in pattern and texture, such as fish, birds, flowers, and reptiles, are highly recommended for this technique. The insect world especially provides a wealth of inspiration for crayon resist projects. Youngsters are often excited by the variety of insects found in their environment and the teacher can stimulate further participation by encouraging them to collect specimens and share them with their classmates. Other sources, such as illustrated books, color slides, and films on insects, will aid in broadening the childrens' awareness of insect life and give them a richer understanding of its limitless variety.

A study of the insect world helps the children in art because in the structure of almost every insect they find various aspects and components of design such as the filigree pattern in the wings of a butterfly, dragonfly or moth, rhythmic segments of a grasshopper's abdomen, contrasting motifs on a cicada's back, simplicity of the symmetrical balance of a ladybug's body, or curvilinear grace of a praying mantis' legs.

In the crayon-resist technique, the patterns and designs of the subject chosen are most important. The different species and sizes of the insects will often guarantee variety in the composition. Usually the more insects the children incorporate in their crayon composition, the richer and more complex the design

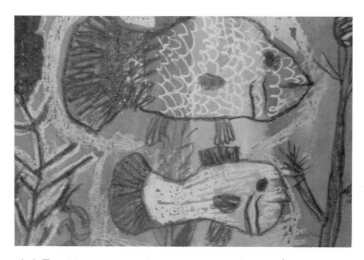

When applying watercolor washes in crayon-resist paintings, remember that the watercolor always appears twice as intense when wet. When dry, its brilliancy often diminishes. Sometimes a second coat of watercolor, after the first application has dried, is recommended. Try giving crayon-resists, crayon-engravings, and oil pastel paintings a coat of polymer medium or glossy finish spray varnish for a glowing, richer color effect.

becomes and subsequently, the negative areas evolve into varied and unique shapes. Background flowers, weeds, grasses, trees, branches, rock formations, webs, vines, and pollen all help tie the composition together.

A successful crayon-resist painting depends on the following technical requirements: the crayon must be applied to the white drawing or light-colored construction paper with a heavy pressure so that the crayon surface will resist the watercolor or tempera paint that is applied in the final stage of the process. A good way to ensure a solid application of crayon is to utilize several layers of newspaper padding under the paper when crayoning. In order to capitalize on the full effect of this medium, the student should plan to leave certain areas of the paper uncrayoned, for example, between two objects, two colors, and object and background, as well as sections within shapes or objects, such as veins within leaves or wings. Negative space can be enriched with pattern of radiating lines, ripples as in a stream, dots, spirals, circles, and wiggly lines.

Encourage the youngsters to be imaginative in their employment of the color crayons. White crayon can be especially effective in this technique. Black crayon provides strong contrast; however, if a final black tempera wash is planned, black crayon should not be employed in the crayoning stage.

When the crayoning is completed, two techniques of resist may be employed—the wet or the dry process. In the dry method, the student paints directly over his crayon composition using watercolor or water-diluted tempera. If the crayon has not been

Children gathered a variety of leaves, drew them in crayon to fill the page in an all-over design, some touching, some overlapping. They employed a heavy, strong pressure when crayoning. Then, using their watercolors and brushes, they applied the flowing watercolor to create a mood of spring or autumn. These colorful designs make effective notebook and container covers.

applied heavily enough (the teacher should check this), the paint will often saturate and obliterate the crayon, but in some instances this situation can be partially corrected by quickly running water over the paper to remove the excess paint. It is highly recommended that the teacher test the viscosity of the tempera paint on a sample crayoned sheet before allowing the children to go ahead with the final painting stage.

In the wet method the desks or tables of a painting area should be covered with newspaper. The children immerse their crayoned paper in water until it is thoroughly wet, then carry it to their desks or painting table. They then load their brushes with watercolor and drop or float the color on the white areas of the paper. They may also let the brush trail around the edges of the crayoned objects and let the paint flow to the center. They may use one wash color for unity or a variety of colors for excitement. The wet process is especially recommended for resist compositions dealing with undersea and aviary themes. Sometimes white areas of the paper left unpainted can be very effective. For a large class the teacher might prepare beforehand several containers of water-diluted tempera or watercolor in assorted hues. A large table or a counter space near a sink could be designated as an area for applying the paint over the crayon compositions.

In addition to the colorful world of insects, the following subjects are recommended for crayon-resist paintings: *Tropical Fish, A Flower Garden, Fireworks Display, The Circus, The Fair, Umbrellas in the Rain, Halloween Parade, Imaginative Designs.*

Steps in a crayon-resist painting. Usually the preliminary crayoning in line only takes one class session, the crayon patterns and selected solid areas a second class period, and the watercoloring a final art class. Check to see that the students use enough water in their watercolor application so that the paint does not obliterate the crayon colors.

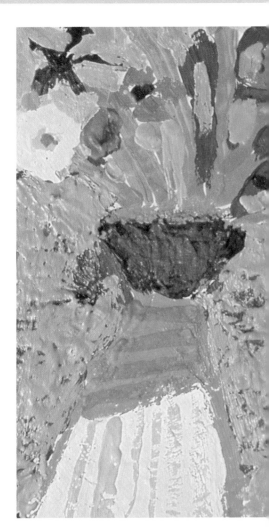

CRAYON ENCAUSTIC

Crayon encaustic may be too pretentious a name for the simple, though exciting, melted-crayon technique described in this chapter. It is, nonetheless, a fascinating new word to add to the children's art vocabulary. The encaustic process is the kind of art adventure that is reserved only for those upper elementary teachers and their young charges who are brave in heart, eager to try something new, and patient enough to salvage a year's supply of broken crayons.

What this project demands more than anything else is a surplus of discarded crayons in all colors. One enthusiastic classroom teacher makes the encaustic painting activity an annual spring event which the children eagerly anticipate. Because the crayons are used throughout the year, this project is suggested as a schoolyear's-end art experience. The technical procedure follows.

Remove paper wrapping from the accumulated crayons, break into small pieces, and place in baby food cans or small juice tins. A muffin tin also works well. It should fit over a deeper and slightly larger baking tin so there is space for water under the muffin tin. Each tin should contain crayons of a different color. Because of space limitations the number of

The beautiful paintings on the facing page were created by employing the melted crayon or encaustic process. The size of the background cardboard, either white or colored, was approximately 9″ × 12″. Color reproductions of flower paintings by noted artists including Odilon Redon, Vincent van Gogh, Paul Ce-zanne, and Paul Gauguin were displayed and referred to during the project. A bouquet of multi-hued anemones provided the immediate motivation. Grade 3. Athens Academy, Athens, Georgia.

colors may have to be curtailed. However, the basic colors plus white, black, pink, blue-green, red-orange, yellow-green, ochre, gray, brown, and tints of blue, green, and purple should be made available.

The most functional working station for an encaustic-painting project is a large newspaper-protected table. Put the narrow end of the table against a wall close to an electrical outlet. Place an electric hot plate in the middle of this table. If necessary, two plates may be used or one plate with two burners.

Put the crayon-filled jars or tins in a 2 or 3 inch deep baking pan. Fill the pan two-thirds full with water and place on the hot plate. Turn on electric current. When crayons have melted, reduce heat and put one or more Q-tips or small watercolor brushes in each container. These should be old brushes, if possible, designated for this project only.

If the hot water in the metal pan is kept at the level of the melted crayon, in the jars or tins, the crayons will keep a flowing painting consistency.

Do not crowd the working area. A limited group of four students, depending on the size of the table, is recommended.

A white or colored cardboard approximately 9 × 12 or 12 × 12 inches is recommended as the painting

Subject matter themes for crayon encaustic paintings are limitless but children seem to respond to motifs such as flowers, butterflies, fish, birds, and, as the illustrations on this page prove, happy circus clowns!

surface. Scrap mat board, chipboard, or grocery carton board coated with latex paint are other possibilities.

A preliminary sketch for a crayon encaustic painting is usually recommended. A flower bouquet, butterfly, exotic bird in foliage, fantastic fish in seaweed, or clown's head are excellent subject matter possibilities.

The teacher must supervise the encaustic painting process rather carefully. *The water must not be allowed to boil out in the pan.* The electric current must be regulated from time to time so the melted crayon does not cool off. Brushes or applicators should not be switched from container to container. Children should take turns with the colors they need.

Caution: Color crayon containers should not be taken out of the heating pan during painting.

This is a project that cannot be rushed. Sometimes the beauty of the encaustic does not materialize until after several layers of crayon have been applied. There will be an exciting impasto quality to the finished work if time is taken. When one color is applied over another, there is the possibility of further embellishment by incising lines with a nail to reveal the color underneath. It is a project full of surprises with a color richness that is unsurpassed!

If the melted crayon layers are applied one over another in the encaustic process, sometimes an unusual color effect can be produced by scratching from one layer down to another with a nail, as seen in the illustrations on this page.

CRAYON ENGRAVING

Crayon engraving, a technique involving the use of crayon and black tempera or poster paint, has become a popular and standard project in many elementary schools, but its many exciting and varied possibilities have not yet been fully explored. Students are too often satisfied with quick, superficial designs or with hasty scribbles and random scratches. New worlds of pattern and texture are yet to be discovered and the combination of crayon engraving with other media, such as oil pastel, to enhance the process invites further investigation.

Basically, the crayon-engraving technique employs a graphic, linear approach. Therefore subject matter or compositions which are rich in line, texture, and pattern are best suited to this medium. Students can turn, for instance, to the natural world for their inspiration: animals such as the porcupine, anteater, armadillo, zebra; birds, especially those of exotic plummage; reptiles such as turtles, iguanas, and horned toads; insects such as dragonflies, praying mantes, butterflies, and beetles; crustaceans such as crabs and crayfish; fish and shells of any species; and to all varieties of plant life.

The preliminary drawing for a crayon engraving should be made in pencil on newsprint or manila paper of the same size as the desired final composition. This will prove helpful especially if the student decides to transfer his drawing.

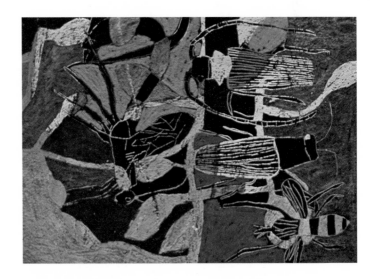

The insect world has unlimited possibilities for creative interpretations as illustrated in these crayon engravings by intermediate grade youngsters. Here, and on facing page, the engravings are embellished in the final stage with an application of oil pastels giving them a glow and vibrancy that is unmatched.

The first step in this technique is to apply varied colors of crayon to the selected paper surface. Recommended paper for this background is a sturdy white drawing or white construction stock. *The crayon should be applied evenly and with strong pressure so that the paper surface is completely covered.* Several layers of newspaper employed as padding during the crayoning will help ensure an even, rich coating of crayon. The youngsters may begin the crayoning phase by first making a scribble design in a light-colored crayon all over the paper and then filling in the resulting shapes solidly with a variety of bright colors; they may apply rich swatches or patches of color that slightly overlap, or they can relate their color areas to coincide with their drawings. A limited or full color range can be employed for the crayon background depending upon the mood or effect desired. In any case, the most intense and most brilliant colors are recommended for the best effects. *Black crayon should not be applied.* Eschew the use, too, of the metallic crayons such as gold, silver, and copper.

After the crayoning has been completed, the surface crayon flecks should be brushed off with a paper towel. *Be sure the children put their names on the back of their crayoned sheets before the tempera coating is applied.* In most instances, black tempera is recommended. The tempera paint, either liquid or powdered (mixed with water), should be the consistency of milk. To make it adhere to the waxy crayoned surface, it must usually be mixed with a very small amount of liquid soap, approximately a tablespoonful to a pint of tempera (or the brush filled with paint can be rubbed over a bar of soap before applying it to the crayoned surface). In any case, it is recommended that the teacher test the paint on a sample sheet of crayoned paper to see if it covers well and can be engraved without chipping.

When the tempera-coated surface is thoroughly dry, the student may transfer his sketch or preliminary line drawing by coating the reverse side of it with white crayon, placing it (crayoned surface down) on the black tempera-coated side and with a sharp pencil or ball-point tip making the transfer. A white transfer paper, which is recommended for this process, is available in art supply stores.

The next step is the actual engraving or incising through the tempera to the crayon. A preliminary outline engraving with a nail is suggested. Be sure the students place protective newspapers on the desk because the engraving can be a slightly messy process.

After a linear composition is achieved, the youngster can delineate the textural or patterned areas using a variety of found tools. High contrast can be achieved by scraping away some areas down to the surface of the crayon with a paring knife or metal nail file.

After the students have completed the engraving processes, they may enrich their composition by applying oil pastel colors over some of the black tempera surfaces. Finally, the composition may be enhanced in many instances by engraving patterns and textural marks through the pasteled areas.

Crayon engraving is a fascinating mixed-media technique that opens new avenues to line, color, pattern, and texture discoveries, especially for the middle and upper grade youngster.

Three stages in a crayon engraving by a primary grade child. Left: The initial engraving with nail through the black tempera to the crayoned surface. Center: The creation of patterns, details, and open crayon areas. Right: The addition of oil pastel colors to enrich the composition.

"Pets and Friends." Grade 1. Ann Arbor, Michigan. There is a delightful freshness and directness in this multicrayon engraving that began with a yellow crayon layer on white oak tag followed by crayon layers of orange, red, and black. The contrasts of dark and light areas achieved through bold directional engraving down to the paper surface are most effective.

MULTICRAYON ENGRAVING

A crayon engraving project that offers special opportunities for unusual color effects is the crayon-over-crayon engraving. For this technique, wax crayons and a sturdy paper with a very slick surface such as oak tag or colored railroad board are required. Newspaper padding should be employed during the crayoning process. All the color crayons can be employed but it is recommended that a limited color sequence be used.

It is advisable to begin with a solid coat of a light crayon such as yellow because a dark initial crayon coat stains the surface of the paper making it difficult to distinguish the subsequently engraved lines. Successive layers of crayon should be applied over the first light-colored coating, building from light to dark. Apply the crayon in short, swift strokes with a definite pressure. You may change the direction of the strokes for better coverage. However, do not exert too much pressure on the crayon, since this tends to break through previous layers. A facial tissue or paper towel may be used to burnish the completed crayoned surface before beginning the engraving process.

Tools found to be most effective for multicrayon engraving include nails, metal nail files, scissor points, compass points, and paring knives. Discarded dental tools and nut picks are recommended, if available.

Turn to the animal and bird world for the most successful multicrayon engraving themes, to creatures such as the armadillo, porcupine, owl, peacock, turtle, zebra, and tiger whose special features and characteristics offer textural and pattern-filled exploitation. Upper grades. Newton, Massachusetts.

Begin the engraving with a nail creating the linear pattern or design. Proceed to scratch out pattern and texture. Finally use a fingernail file or paring knife to scrape out solid areas allowing the marks of the cutting tool to show.

For children in the primary grades a small crayoning surface is recommended. Use oak tag in 9 × 12 or 12 × 12 inch sizes. Although the crayon application is time-consuming and young children have a limited working span, they tackle the technique with enthusiasm. The crayon overlays may range from yellow to orange to red to brown to black or from yellow to green to blue to blue-violet to black. You may alternate cool and warm colors in succeeding layers.

In the intermediate or upper grades, a large sheet of oak tag or colored railroad board (12 × 18 or 12 × 12 inches) may be introduced.

Multicrayon engraving adds an exciting dimension to the potential of the common crayon. It unfolds new horizons of color exploitation for the elementary school youngster.

OIL PASTEL

The various brands of oil pastel now on the art market have opened up a whole new world of color expression in the elementary art program. They are available in a wide range of hues and are generally within the budget range of most schools. Their most attractive feature is the ease with which young children can apply them to obtain rich, glowing colors.

Their only drawback, if any, is that they have a tendency to stain; youngsters should be cautioned to protect their clothes when they use oil pastels.

Colored construction paper is highly recommended as a background surface for oil pastel paintings. In most instances a preliminary sketch in white chalk or light pastel is suggested.

One very successful approach in creating paintings with oil pastels (see flower composition on facing page) is to make the preliminary line drawing in black felt-nib ink marker on colored construction paper and then apply the oil pastel so that the initial

black sketch line remains to unify the composition. In most instances this technique produces echoes of stained-glass window vibrancy.

Children should be encouraged to use the pastel colors boldly and imaginatively, pressing hard to achieve the richest, most vibrant effects. They should be guided to color objects or shapes from the inside out rather than rigidly outlining a shape in one color and coloring in another. Suggest that they juxtapose light colors next to dark colors for exciting contrast. They should be challenged to repeat colors. to use white, gray, and black for contrasting effects, and encouraged to exploit the background paper color, allowing it to show between patterned areas to achieve unity. Pastel may be applied over pastel for unusual color nuances. If they wish to lighten a color deemed too dark, they can apply white pastel over it to change its value. Applying the pastels impressionistically in dots or small strokes on colored construction paper is another novel technique youngsters enjoy.

Facing page: *A collection of butterflies provided the inspiration for this oil pastel. Grade 4. This page: Space ships and astronauts was the theme for this intermediate grade art project. A number of students contributed to a group mural while others in the class chose to make individual oil pastel compositions.*

OIL PASTEL RESIST

Teachers familiar with crayon resist technique will welcome oil pastel as a resist medium because it does not require the high consumption of time and the intense exertion on the part of the children that the rich application of crayon demands.

Basically the same steps as crayon resist are followed. A preliminary drawing in white or yellow chalk is made on colored construction paper. Ask the children to vary the chalk lines from thick to thin. The pastel is then applied with heavy pressure so it will resist the final coat of paint. The chalk lines should not be colored or covered. Some of the paper should remain uncovered between pasteled areas, objects and background, and patterns. The brightest, lightest values of pastel are generally recommended. White and gray oil pastel may be used. Black oil pastel should not be employed since the final resist effect will be achieved by an application of black paint.

Oil pastel resist: Steps in the process. Top: *Preliminary drawing in white chalk on colored construction paper.* Center: *Oil pastel applied in solid areas and patterns without covering the chalk lines.* Bottom: *Black tempera paint brushed over the oil pastel composition. Paint may have to be slightly diluted with water.*

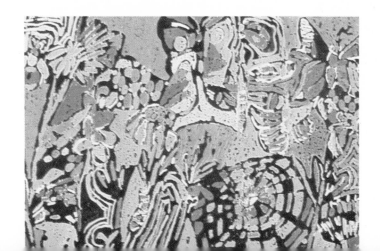

Check the completed pastel composition for: variety of colors, repetition of colors, pattern, or texture (exploit a variety of pattern: dots, circles overlapping, wiggly jigsaw lines, radiating lines, ripple lines as seen surrounding a pebble in a stream, hatch and cross-hatch lines, stars, asterisks, diamonds, spirals), varied open spaces of uncolored paper, and solid application of pastel before applying the tempera.

Place the pastel composition on a newspaper-protected surface and gently apply a coat of black tempera paint with large watercolor brush. Let the brush float over the surface of the paper. A word of caution: *Always try the paint first on a sample pastel-colored sheet of paper.* If it covers the pastel, it is too thick. Dilute slightly with water. Remember that the resisting oil in the oil pastels dries out shortly after application; don't wait too long before the over-painting.

Oil pastel resists may be given a coat of clear shellac or varnish when completely dry to bring out their beauty.

Imaginary animal themes inspired these fantastic oil pastel resist paintings by fourth and fifth grade children. Youngsters respond to the unusual compositional challenges these make-believe creatures present.

Vegetables and fruit cut in half provide exciting radiating design motifs to use in art projects. Tropical fish, seaweed, and shells are also excellent themes for oil pastel resists. See the beautiful marine interpretation by a fourth grade youngster on page 142.

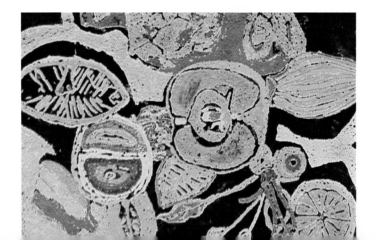

COLLAGE

One of the most exciting and popular forms of visual expression in elementary schools today is the art of collage.

A half-century ago shocking dismay greeted the intial collages of Pablo Picasso, Georges Braque, and Kurt Schwitters. Today their creations in paste (the word collage derives from the French *coller*—to paste), paper, and other discards from the wastebasket appear relatively tame. The well-springs from which today's collagists draw their materials is so bountiful in content and variety that there are practically no limits to contemporary collage or assemblage expression.

There are many approaches to the art of collage. They range from simple cutting and pasting of colored paper or cloth to complex sewing, shearing, and gluing of plastics, plywood, and cardboard. Some recommended materials for elementary school col-

"On Our Street" was the subject of this colorful collage by a first grade child. A preliminary discussion centered around houses, churches, stores, trees, bushes, sidewalks, cars, trucks, telephone poles, traffic signs, pet dogs and cats, and other ordinary, everyday neighborhood sights. The sun "just happened."

lage are colored poster and construction paper, fluorescent and day-glo paper, cloth remnants, found materials, wallpaper and rug samples, multicolored tissue paper, plus colored sections and ads from magazines.

Children of all ages enjoy cutting, tearing, and pasting, so teachers will find the collage project a most effective avenue for teaching the many elements of composition: variety of shapes, overlapping to create unity and subtle depth, positive and negative space concepts, color contrast and relationships, balance pattern, and emphasis. The fact that the objects or shapes the youngster cuts out can be shifted or changed before he decides on the final arrangement gives him and the teacher a welcome opportunity to discuss the composition before he pastes the separate pieces permanently.

Teachers will find many of the following suggestions useful in helping children with their collage expressions.

Cut and arrange the big shapes of your composition first.

If you are using a colored background, be sure to exploit it in your design. Let some of the color background show to help unify your composition.

Try different materials for the background surface: chipboard, oak tag, plywood, burlap, corrugated board, railroad or posterboard, wallpaper book samples.

Small details or pattern can be pasted on the large shapes before the large shapes are adhered to the background surface.

The wonderful thing about cut-and-paste projects is that youngsters can arrange the separate shapes in all kinds of configurations before they decide where they finally want them. It is recommended that preliminary drawings for collage projects not be required in the primary grades. The separate parts, however, may be drawn before being cut out.

Overlapping of shapes can be exploited in the collage technique more successfully than in any other art form. As children mature, they can be guided to see the unusual shapes and the suggestion of depth they can create through overlapping.

Some eye-catching materials such as aluminum foil, shiny plastic, and cellophane have a strong fascination for children and, if not properly guided, they are apt to use them in an unrestrained manner. Suggest their utilization as elements of emphasis.

Repetition of a color, shape, value, or pattern can help give unity to a collage; however, instead of repeating an element, color, or shape in the same intensity or size, change it slightly when repeating it for variety.

Recommend the use of uneven rather than an even number of repeated elements; for example, repeat a certain shape or color three times rather than twice.

Encourage the use of informal rather than formal balance in collage compositions.

Avoid a lot of "sticky" problems by using a discarded magazine as a paste-applying surface. When children need a clean pasting area, they just turn to another page in the magazine.

(See Appendix E for a list of materials useful in collage projects.)

Facing page: *Motivational inspiration and the resulting collages.* This page: *Cloth remnants add a new dimension to collage creations. Affinitive materials include yarn, ric rac, fringes, and buttons.*

TISSUE PAPER COLLAGE

On the first day of a tissue-collage project the teacher might surprise the class by opening or unfolding a package of assorted color tissue papers. The excitement grows as tissue overlays tissue on white paper or against a window while the children are invited to choose the overlapping colors and to identify the resulting hues.

To encourage color awareness and color exploration, the free-design colored tissue collage is recommended for children of all ages. Using a sheet of oak tag, white drawing, or light-colored construction paper as a background surface, the youngsters cut or tear different colors, sizes, and shapes of tissue and adhere them to the white background with liquid laundry starch, overlapping the various shapes as they proceed. The teacher should suggest that they begin with the lighter colored tissues first and progress to darker values. It is difficult to change the

Illustration top left shows colored crayons employed as a linear unifying composition for a colored tissue paper collage. Center: Liquid laundry starch was the adhesive used to apply the tissue. Bottom: Black permanent ink felt-nib pen was utilized here for the initial drawing. Nonpermanent inks bleed when starch paste is used.

value of the dark colors by overlapping. It is recommended that the dark color tissue paper be reserved for the second phase of the pasting.

It is also recommended that the children first apply starch to the area they wish to cover with the tissue. Then the tissue piece should be placed down carefully over the moistened area and another coat of starch applied over it. Use a large watercolor or half-inch utility brush to apply the starch. Brushes may be cleaned with water. Be sure that all loose edges of tissue are glued down carefully. Discarded half-pint milk cartons are excellent to use for the starch containers.

As the children build and extend their compositions to the borders of the page, encourage them to look for unusual hidden shapes of animals, birds, insects, fish, or fantastic figures. Once a form emerges and is identified, it can be clarified by adding torn pieces or strips of tissue in deeper colors to suggest or indicate arms, legs, horns, beaks, tails, hats, fins, and other appendages to give it significant character.

To emphasize the positive shapes, the background may be subdued by applying gray or white tissue over it. Crayons, felt-nib pens, colored felt markers, or tempera paint in white, gray, and black can be used to add exciting linear delineation to the shape where desired, such as bark on a tree, scales on a fish, feathers on a bird, hair on an animal, or veins in a leaf. As an alternative, the positive shapes may remain unembellished while the background can be enriched with detail, pattern, and texture for contrast.

This free-design approach with tissue is only one of

many avenues open to children who wish to create in colored tissue. Another recommended technique utilizes a preliminary drawing made with black or dark-color crayons, waterproof felt-nib pen, or felt marker on white drawing or construction paper or tagboard. After the drawing is completed, the cut or torn tissue is applied (as suggested earlier) to create the color effect. It is recommended that light-color tissue be used first and that pieces be cut or torn slightly larger than the shape drawn. When too dark a color of tissue is applied, the preliminary line drawing is often obscured. However, when the tissue composition dries, some of these lines may be accented or emphasized by redrawing them. Colored tissue used in conjunction with color patterned ads from magazines is also a very effective collage medium.

One last reminder. The storage of new and used tissue is a critical consideration. Tissue wrinkles and crumples very easily, compounding storage problems. Encourage students to store it flat in designated boxes or drawers. Always allow a liberal amount of time for cleanup and storage procedures.

These colored tissue compositions began as free form collages. The youngsters cut or tore the tissue and applied it in overlapping stages to create an abstract design. When dry they used black and colored felt-nib markers searching for and emphasizing realistic shapes. Some children used brushes and paint. One

word of caution bears repetition: suggest that the students use the light values of tissue first and, when necessary, overlap tissue to create darker values. A dark color tissue is difficult to change if a light value is desired later. In a quandary, paste white paper over the area and start again.

MOSAICS

The multifaceted technique of mosaic art, with its color segments called *tesserae*, has found its way into the elementary art program to enrich the design experiences of children. It is a welcome albeit challenging addition to the repertoire of child art expression. It requires a longer time allotment, supplemental storage, children with persistence, and a teacher with sympathetic patience. Youngsters can have success with the mosaic technique employing such simple materials as colored construction paper, paste, and scissors.

The background surface for a paper mosaic can be any of the following materials: construction paper in assorted colors, railroad board, chipboard, illustration board, oak tag, or discarded gift box covers. The adhesive employed may be wheat paste, slightly water-diluted school paste, white glue, or rubber cement. Mosaic, left, has tesserae of vinyl and linoleum glued to a Masonite board. Grade 6.

Motivation for the project might include visits to contemporary mosaic mural installations in churches, civic centers, hospitals, hotels, banks, schools, or business offices. Color films and slides that deal with mosaic art, past and present, including San Vitale in Rome, Gaudi's Cathedral in Barcelona, and Rodia's Watts Towers in Los Angeles, should be shown if possible. Subject matter for mosaics that is simple, yet exciting enough to interest young children, includes: *Birds of Plumage, Fish in the Sea, Animals and Their Habitats, Flower Gardens* and *Butterflies*.

In mosaic design, as in all two-dimensional art expression, an important initial step is the preliminary sketch made from nature, from visits to natural museums, or from reference to films, slides, and photographs. These sketches are then developed into a satisfactory composition the size of the actual mosaic desired. Colored construction paper, railroad board in assorted colors, and chipboard or oak tag can be utilized for the background surface.

In the drawing, usually one subject is emphasized but aspects of secondary emphasis through repetition of the main motif, though on a smaller scale, may be included. The children should be encouraged to see and delineate characteristic features such as beaks, eyes and claws on birds, horns on animals, and fins and gills on fish.

One of the most critical factors in the success of a mosaic project is the effective organization of materials and tools. There must be an adequate supply of tesserae. In the case of colored construction paper, narrow strips of paper can be precut and stored according to color in shoe boxes. Suggested adhe-

sives for paper mosaic include water-diluted school paste, wheat paste, or white liquid glue.

During a mosaic project, students should be instructed to take turns selecting the desired color strips or individual tessera from the supply-table boxes. They may begin by pasting tessera on a general area such as the sky or ground or they may concentrate first on a significant feature of the main figure—the beak of a bird, the horns of an animal, or the pattern in a butterfly wing. They should be guided to employ a varied application of the tesserae instead of a precise, brick-laying technique. The open spaces left between tesserae should vary somewhat for best effects. Tesserae should not touch or overlap each other, if possible.

Tesserae should not be cut in exactly the same size. It will help if the paper strips, originally cut, vary in width from ¼ to ¾ inch. These may then be cut in squares, rectangles, or triangles.

Youngsters may create excitement in their mosaics through a contrast of tesserae colors in the various areas—the wing of a bird against the body, the stamen against the flower petal, an insect on a leaf. An important strategy in achieving mosaic quality is to employ several values of colored tesserae in the larger areas; for example, two or three kinds of blue in the sky, several greens in the grass or leaves and many kinds of brown, umber, ochre for earth and tree trunk tones. The brightest, most intense colors can be reserved for rich emphasis, for example the beak or claw of a bird, horns of a bull, eyes of a cat, or stamen of a flower.

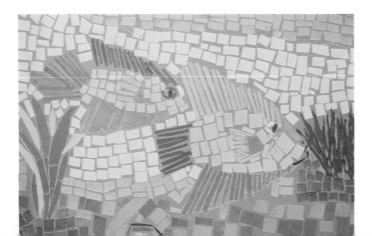

Underwater themes are especially effective for mosaic compositions because of the variety of shapes found in fish, shells, and seaweed. These beautifully space-filled compositions are by upper grade youngsters. Oshkosh, Wisconsin.

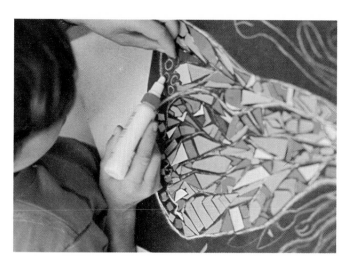

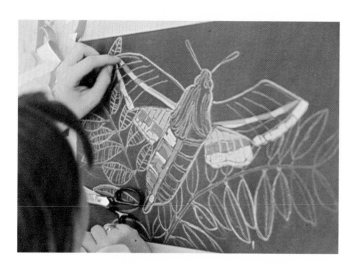

VEGETABLE PRINTS

Printmaking projects should be carefully pro-grammed by the teacher so that they range from simple processes in the primary grades to complex techniques in the upper grades. Some of the most colorful, most exciting prints can be made by very young children employing vegetables, as well as found objects such as buttons, flat wooden clothes pins, wooden spools, bottle caps, mailing tubes, sponges, and corks.

Cord can be glued to the top of a bottle cap in a free design for a printing stamp. Assorted vegetables and fruit (okra, peppers, carrots, mushrooms, oranges, artichokes, cabbage) can be cut in half, painted, and printed. The excitement grows when the students discover, perhaps for the first time, the beauty of the hidden design in these natural forms. The halved vegetables or fruit are coated on the cut surface with tempera paint or pressed on a tempera-

Vegetable prints may be embellished by the application of oil pastels as shown in illustrations left. Top: A youngster applies the pastel colors between the printed shapes allowing some of the background paper to show. Note in bottom illustration how the employment of the colored pastels has enriched the vegetable print shown at center.

moistened folded paper towel and then printed on a sheet of colored construction paper to form a repeat or free design.

The most popular of the vegetable-print projects exploit the common potato as a printing stamp. The potato is cut in half with a paring knife and the flat surface is incised to create a relief. Children must be cautioned to exercise caution when using vegetable cutting tools. Recommended tools for use are small scissors, metal fingernail files, and assorted nails. Melon ball scoops, if available, are excellent for creating circular designs. In the upper grades paring knives may be introduced if employed with extreme care.

Youngsters should be encouraged to aim for a bold, simple breakup of space in their cutout or incised designs. Suggest the exploitation of cross-cuts, wedges as in a pie, assorted sized holes, star, sunburst, and spiderweb effects, always keeping negative and positive design factors in mind.

The vegetables must be fresh, crisp, and solid for controlled carving, cutting, and printing and should be refrigerated between art sessions. A number of methods may be utilized to ink the cut vegetables, including direct brush application with tempera or watercolor. Try using a tempera-saturated printing pad made of several thicknesses of paper toweling or water-soluble printing ink on a Masonite sheet, discarded serving tray, or cookie tin.

Construction paper in assorted colors is perhaps the most popular and most effective surface for vegetable printing, although other papers including colored tissue, cream or gray manila, and wallpaper

---

Vegetable print all-over or repeat designs make excellent covers for notebooks, pencil holders (recycle a soup can) and household dispensers. To protect the work apply a coat of clear shellac or plastic spray.

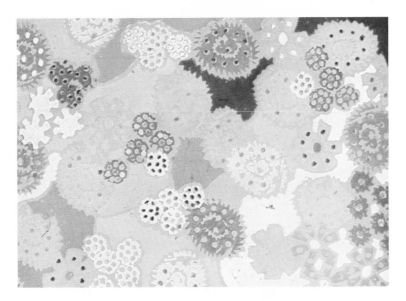 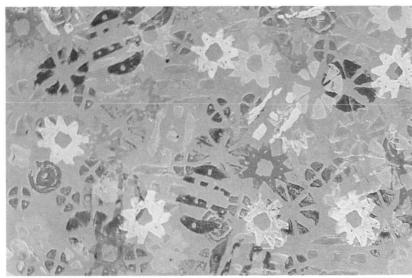

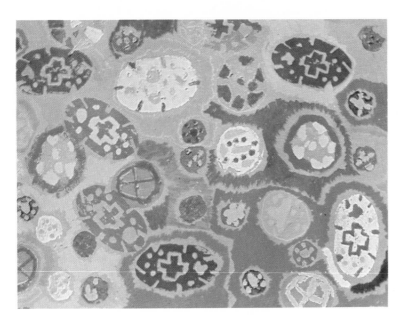 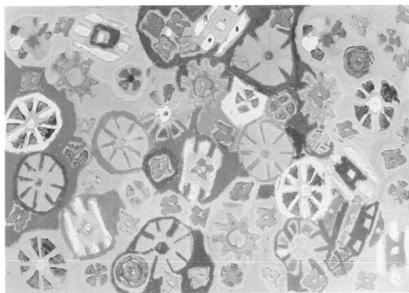

have been successfully used. A few practice applications of the vegetable stamp on scrap sheets of colored construction paper are recommended. In some vegetable print projects children might be guided to develop a definite repeat pattern. Suggest they repeat the same motif in the same color in several places on their paper allowing some prints to go off the page to suggest continuity. This repetition of a motif creates unity. In other instances the design can be left to the child's own inventiveness but discourage rushing just to finish. Very often the imperfection of the youngster's effort lends a naive, spontaneous quality to the design. The children will discover that by sharing their vegetable and found object stamps they can often produce exciting variations in their patterns and designs.

Vegetable prints have artistic merit in their simplest form, but they can often be embellished with other media to add richness and variety. One of the most successful of these augmentations is the application of varicolored oil pastel to the negative spaces between the printed shapes of the vegetables. Unity can be achieved by retaining some of the background colored construction paper between the pasteled areas and the printed shapes. Older students can carry the vegetable-print technique into even more complex undertakings by combining it with colored tissue overlays.

Vegetable and found objects prints make excellent covers for notebooks and pencil containers (adhere the printed paper to a discarded soup can). Protect the surface with a coat of clear shellac or varnish.

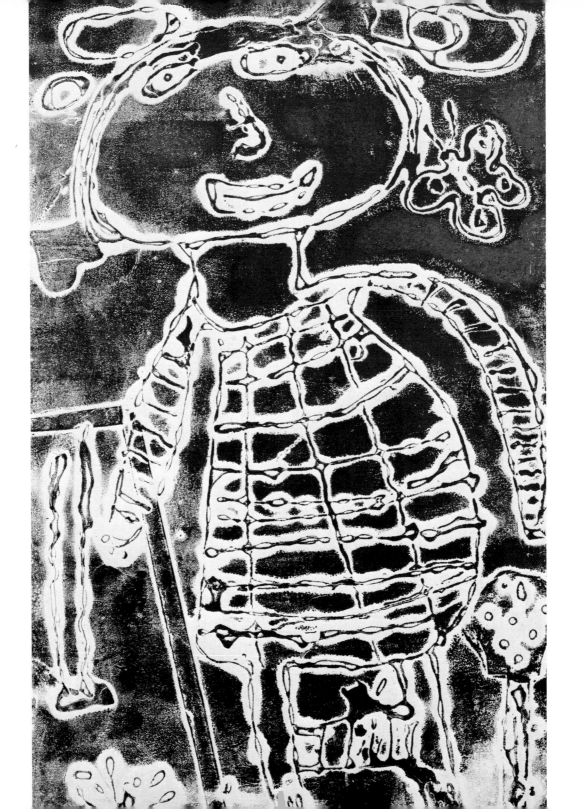

GLUE LINE RELIEF PRINTS

A printmaking approach that is remarkably successful in all grades is the applied-glue-line-on-cardboard print. It is a relatively simple technique but requires at least two separate studio sessions because the glue must dry throughly before inking can be done. The youngsters will probably have to take their turns during the inking and printing stages, but a wise teacher will plan other creative assignments for those who are waiting at their desks.

Materials required are a smooth-surfaced cardboard (discarded glossy-surfaced box covers are excellent) or tagboard for the printing plate (plate sizes recommended are 9 × 9 inch, 9 × 12 inch, 12 × 12 inch); white liquid glue in the smallest plastic container with nozzle; water soluble ink (black is suggested); a *soft rubber* roller or brayer for inking; and an inking surface such as a 12-inch square of tempered Masonite, a sheet of wax paper stretched and taped over a piece of plywood, or a discarded cookie tin; and newsprint or colored tissue paper to print on.

Facing page: *Glue line relief print, 12″ × 18″. A self-portrait by a first grade child. Oshkosh, Wisconsin.* This page: *Same technique, same size print by a sixth grade youngster. Note that the printing ink covers parts of the background as well as the glue lines themselves.*

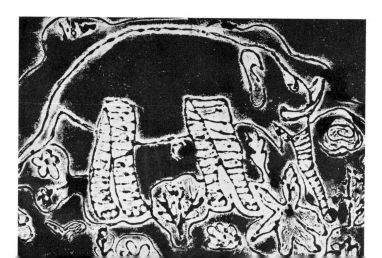

Subject matter possibilities for glue prints are found everywhere. Young children will respond to birds, fish, flowers, insects, and animals as motifs. Students in the upper grades may choose more complex, legendary, Biblical, historical, or space-science themes as well as still-life or cityscape compositions, portraits, or figure studies.

A preliminary drawing is definitely recommended. Suggest to the children that they keep the drawing bold and simple, if possible. They should minimize the very minute, intricate details that a pencil can make but which unfortunately will blend together in the glue application and are often lost in the printing. On a 12-inch square cardboard it is wiser for the youngsters to limit themselves to one large motif (bird, fish, animal, insect) and its complementary foliage rather than attempting several smaller shapes. In this way children can clearly delineate the characteristic features of eye, beak, claw, feather, or scale with the flowing glue. Always evaluate the composition with the youngsters for a space-filling design, variety of shapes, exciting pattern, and avenues leading into the composition.

The cardboard plate is now ready for the application of the liquid glue. Holding the nozzle point of the glue container against the cardboard, gently squeeze the container trailing the glue over the drawn line. With older children the teacher may suggest that the thickness of the glue line be varied by controlling the pressure on the container, but in most instances a linear variety is achieved naturally because it is difficult to manage a steady flow of glue.

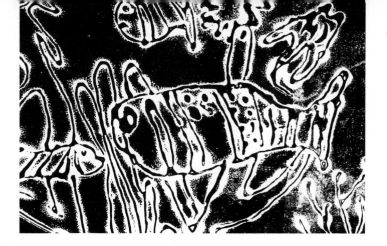

The glue must be allowed to dry thoroughly before the cardboard plate can be inked. Some teachers suggest an overnight drying period. Designate an inking and printing station in the room. This could be a table or counter generously protected by newspapers. Demonstrate the application of the glue, the inking, printing, and wet-print storing procedures for the entire class. This will save a lot of time usually spent in giving individual instructions. When completely dry the white glue becomes transparent.

Squeeze out a ribbon of water-base printing ink on the inking slab. Roll out ink with brayer. Keep rolling until ink is tacky, then apply to the plate with a strong pressure. It is recommended that students stand during this procedure. Roll ink on plate in both directions to be sure all parts of the plate are inked thoroughly. Then remove inked plate to the newspaper-covered printing station. Place a sheet of newsprint or colored tissue paper (slightly larger than the plate) over the plate carefully and apply pressure with the palm of the hand, beginning in the center of the plate and smoothing out toward the edges.

The most exciting glue prints are those in which the inked areas of the plate background as well as those of the glue lines are captured in the final print. To do this the youngster must use fingers, thumb, and heel of hand to press down on the paper between the raised glue lines as the print is taken. For a demonstration print, the teacher should use white or light-colored tissue because the children can see the actual absorption of the ink into the paper and can detect areas that need more pressure to be effective.

The glue line plate itself can be framed and displayed. Give it a coat of colored or metal-patina printing ink. It can be stained with commercial patinas as well. It can also be covered with heavy duty aluminum foil for a stunning effect. See the section on "Aluminum Foil Reliefs."

COLLOGRAPHS

When youngsters reach the intermediate and upper grade levels, they become interested in and challenged by more complex, more technically demanding approaches to printmaking. Cardboard prints, sometimes referred to as collographs (a combination of collage and graph), which can be created with commonly available materials and simple, nonhazardous tools offer this kind of variety, excitement, and exploitation. The final results are often similar to wood or linoleum block prints. The flexibility of rearranging or changing the composition of the print before the final gluing of the separate cardboard shapes in an especially welcome feature of this print technique.

The following materials and tools are required: a piece of cardboard (the lid or bottom section of a shirt or stationery box, chipboard, railroad board, or heavy tagboard), glue, scissors, assorted weight pa-

Facing page and at left: *Steps in the process of making a collograph print. Grade 3.*

pers and cardboards, paper punch, soft rubber brayer or roller, water-soluble printing ink (black is recommended), newsprint paper or colored tissue, shellac, utility brush, and solvent for shellac.

Subject matter themes for cardboard prints are limitless, though the animal world is a favorite. However, there should be the same concern for a strong composition that is given to any other graphic design project. Especially important is the emphasis on effective utilization of a variety of cutout shapes to fill the space of the cardboard the child has chosen. A recommended printing plate size for this intermediate age group is a sheet 9 × 9 inches, 9 × 12 inches, or 12 × 12 inches. Plates much larger than this create a management problem in crowded classes, especially during the inking, printing, and drying phases. Storage of work in progress is a critical factor. The use of large envelopes or folders labeled with the child's name is recommended during the early cutting and gluing stage.

When the youngsters have drawn and cut out the separate, individual shapes from tagboard, manila, corrugated paper, and assorted weight papers and have created open patterns in some of these shapes employing the paper punch and single-edge razor blades (caution: wrap the blade securely with masking tape so that only a small cutting point protrudes at one end), they arrange these elements on the background sheet until a satisfactory composition is obtained. Some pieces may overlap each other for unity and interest; however, the relief should not be built up too high if a successful print is desired. When the students, with the teacher's guidance, achieve satisfy-

ing, space-filling designs, they carefully glue the separate cutout pieces to the plate surface beginning with the first layer shapes. It is very important that all edges of applied pieces be glued down very securely. The whole composition is then given a coat of shellac to seal it, thus preventing the separately-glued pieces from dissolving and coming loose during the printing or cleaning phases. A separate table or counter covered with newspapers should be designated as a shellac-application area. Store shellacked plates out of the students' way, preferably in a well-ventilated area, and allow to dry thoroughly.

Youngster, using his pencil sketch as a guide, glues shapes cut out of oak tag to a more sturdy cardboard for his collograph printing plate. See complete print above..

The inking and printing phase of this project is naturally the most exciting stage for the youngsters, but unless the teacher has planned this segment of the process carefully, it can develop into chaotic bedlam.

The teacher should have on hand several inking surfaces (foot square pieces of tempered Masonite, discarded cookie tins, or cafeteria trays), *soft rubber brayers or ink rollers, three or more inches wide, black water-soluble printing ink, newsprint, poster paper, or colored tissue paper.*

In a typical classroom situation, it is suggested that an inking and printing table covered with newspapers be set up where three to four students can stand and work comfortably. Roll the ink carefully on the plate in both directions using an even, strong pressure.

"The Jungle." Group project collograph by intermediate grade class. Paper punch was used to make holes in some of the oak tag shapes before adhering them. Pinking shears were also employed in some instances.

Take the inked plate to a clean table or desk surface. Place a sheet of newsprint over the inked plate and rub with the palm of the hand.

Use fingers or heel of hand to press corners, edges, and areas between the pasted shapes. Where you want print to be dark, press hardest. Do not wait too long to remove print from plate. Water-soluble inks dry quickly and the paper may stick to the plate. Lift newsprint off carefully and store to dry. All wet prints should be put on shelves, spring-clipped to a clothes-line, or lined along the counters or baseboards where youngsters will not disturb them.

The process of inking and pulling a print should be demonstrated step-by-step for the whole class so that it does not have to be repeated for each student in turn. Additional prints may be made at a later date from a plate that has been inked and has dried thoroughly. Plates need not be washed between printing sessions.

Finished prints can be attractively mounted for display purposes. Children may exchange prints. The plate itself can be inked in two or three colors, mounted, framed, and displayed. It can also be covered with heavy duty aluminum foil. See the Section "Aluminum Foil Relief."

Children in the fifth and sixth grades can exploit the cardboard print technique even further through the use of variety of materials to create linear and textural print quality. Suggested effects include decorative tape, string, gummed reinforcements, textured wall paper, liquid glue lines, plus a variety of found objects.

Illustrations on this page beginning at top: *the cardboard plate, the collograph print, and the aluminum foil relief over the collograph plate. Grade 2. See next four pages for a complete description of the new and exciting aluminum foil relief technique.* Facing page: *Collograph. Grade 6, Japan.*

ALUMINUM FOIL RELIEF

The aluminum foil relief over collage, collograph plate, or glue line relief plate is an exciting new art technique that children in the upper grades will definitely enjoy.

Materials you will need include *heavy duty* household aluminum foil, blunt-point pencils, *soft rubber* brayer or inking roller, white glue, gold patina (either Rub'n'Buff or Treasure Gold), water soluble printing ink (black), and newspapers for protection of working surfaces.

If you have been making prints from your collograph or glue line plate (this should be on a cardboard thicker than oak tag; if not, you can glue the oak tag plate to a thicker sheet of cardboard for this project) and while the ink is still wet on your plate from your last print, cover it with a sheet of foil slightly larger than the plate itself so you can overlap the foil on the back. Do not overlap until you have stretched the foil securely over the plate using your palms from the

The aluminum foil relief as illustrated on this and facing pages is an exciting metal embossing adventure which has untold possibilities for exploitation in the elementary art program, especially at the upper grade level. It utilizes everyday household heavy-duty *foil instead of expensive metal sheeting. The glowing finished product belies the usual expectations of the material. A sure winner!*

center out. If you own a *soft* rubber brayer, roll it over the foil with a strong definite pressure. Now overlap the *excess* foil and secure with masking tape on the back. Remember, shiny surface of the foil up.

Note: If you have not made a print from your plate or the ink has already dried, either apply a fresh coat of printing ink or a coat of white glue to the plate before covering it with the foil. This will stabilize the foil so it will not shift during the indenting process that follows next.

Now using a *blunt pointed* pencil (the big kindergarten pencils are best) press into the foil along both edges of the glue line and along the edges of cardboard shapes to accent the relief. Be careful not to puncture the foil. *Be sure the pencil point is blunt.* Next enrich your relief by indenting the foil with the pencil point to create additional patterns and texture such as veins in leaves, feathers in a bird, bark in trees, ripples in a stream, scales on fish, and grass. You may also incorporate a variety of invented patterns such as hatching, crosshatching, dots, dots within circles, circles, triangles or diamond shapes touching each other, wiggling, rippling, or radiating lines, asterisks, stars, or spirals.

When you have completed this embellishment of the foil, you may pull prints from it. Apply water soluble printing ink to the foil surface with a brayer so that the whole plate is covered except for the deep indentations. It is recommended that the children

Steps in a foil relief. Top: *The pencil drawing on sturdy cardboard. Avoid tiny details because they are often lost in the glue application.* Center: *Applying the glue over the pencil lines. Allow glue to dry completely until transparent.* Bottom: *Inking the glue line plate. Use* soft rubber brayer *and much pressure so that the whole surface is inked.*

stand when they do this because much pressure is needed. Take the inked plate to a clean area. Place a sheet of newsprint or colored tissue paper (slightly larger than the plate) over the inked foil and press with palms, fingers, and soft rubber roller. Remember to press along the edges or borders of the plate if you want a good print. Peel paper off plate gently. You can partially lift paper to see if your print is clear before pulling it off completely.

While the ink is still moist on the foil-covered plate use flat paper towels to wipe it off the raised foil surface until it is shiny and clean. A slightly moist flat folded paper towel will help at first but finish the wiping and polishing with a *dry* paper towel. The ink should remain in the indentations.

Finally you can enrich your aluminum foil relief by applying a patina of gold Rub'n'Buff or Treasure Gold to selected raised surfaces. Apply sparingly with the tip of your finger. In some cases color may be introduced by using oil paint but this should be employed discriminatingly because it can be overdone. Your aluminum foil should not look like an oil painting—the foil should glow through the colors to be most effective. If you apply too much gold or too much color you can remove the excess with a paper towel moistened with turpentine. Use turpentine, too, to clean the metal patina paste off your fingers. Aluminum foil reliefs can be attractively mounted or framed.

Top: *The print from the glue line plate.* Center: *The aluminum foil, shiny side up, is secured with glue or printing ink to the plate and indentations are made with a blunt-point pencil. At this stage a print may be made.* Bottom: *After last print wipe off surface ink from the foil with a slightly moist paper towel. If desired, apply gold Rub 'n' Buff to selected relief surfaces.*

Sketching field trips to a natural history museum provided the subject matter for this beautifully detailed lineolum block print by a fifth grade youngster, Iowa City, Iowa. Separate drawings were made of the mounted animals, then combined in a satisfying composition.

LINOLEUM PRINTS

A technically challenging form of graphic expression recommended for children in the upper elementary grades is linoleum block printing, sometimes referred to as lino printing. Unmounted, gray pliable linoleum suggested for this project may be obtained from art supply firms. In some instances it is available from furniture or department stores but the teachers should make certain it is the pliable kind that can be easily cut and not the brittle, hard-surfaced plastic type. The basic materials and tools needed include a set of lino cutting gouges, a rubber brayer (ink roller), an inking surface, printing ink (water-soluble), and assorted papers such as colored construction, tissue, newsprint, brown wrapping, classified sections of newspapers, wallpaper, and colored pages from magazines. A special inking and printing station covered with newspapers should be provided in the classroom.

Prints on this page are by Japanese children. Grades 4 and 5. Note how much was observed and recorded in these space-filled woodblock prints. Printmaking incorporating woodcutting tools is introduced in the third grade in Japanese schools.

The line print may be often enhanced by printing over colorful magazine ads or colored tissue collage as illustrated here. Heavy pressure must be employed when making the print on tissue backgrounds to make a successful impression. The tissue application may be a free color design or planned to coincide with the blockprint. Remember the composition will be reversed when printed.

Busy upper grade youngsters are in the process of making a reduction linoleum print. The students first cut away selected sections of the linoleum and pulled a number of prints in a red printing ink. While these prints were drying, the students gouged away additional areas of the block. The plate was inked a second time in green and printed over the red edition. Care was taken to register or match the second printing over the first. While these two-color prints dried, the youngsters cut away the final selected areas, then used black ink for their third and last impression. Oshkosh, Wisconsin.

Preliminary drawings and sketches in pencil, black crayon, pen and ink, brush and ink, white crayon on black paper, or felt-nib ink marker are important requisites for a successful printmaking project because they often determine the final composition, including the dark and light pattern, variety of textural exploitation, areas of emphasis, and lines of motion.

The teacher and the students must be cognizant of the fact that each particular lino gouge makes a different cut and although it does not lend itself to the same control as the pencil or pen, it often produces linear effects that are more direct and dynamic. The various gouges, from veiners to scoops and shovels, should be exploited to the fullest extent to achieve both linear and mass effects.

Subject matter themes for lino prints are unlimited, but students will discover rich sources for exciting compositions and textural exploitation in rare birds, jungle animals, insects, fish, old houses, cityscapes, legendary or mythological figures, portraits, and still-life arrangements composed of sports equipment, musical instruments, plants, lanterns, antiques, household utensils, and similar items.

After preliminary sketches have been made, the youngsters may use them as a reference to draw directly on the lino plate or they may transfer their sketch to the lino surface with carbon paper. They should be reminded that the final prints are always the reverse of the sketch especially if they plan to use numerals or letters in their designs. They may, if they wish, reverse their sketches before transferring them to the plate. If the lino surface is a dark color, it may be painted with white paint before the sketch is transferred to the block. Place the sketch, pencil-side down, on the block and rub over it with a metal spoon. The final print will then be compositionally the same as the sketch.

There are various methods recommended for cutting the lino block. The veiners or v-shaped gouges #1 and #2 are suggested to make the initial outlines of the composition. Another approach is to use the scoop or shovel gouges working from the inside of the shapes, thus minimizing tightly outlined compositions.

Sometimes the student can prevent mistakes in cutting by marking an "X" on those areas of the block that are to be gouged out. It is recommended that the youngster employ directional gouge cuts by following the contour of the object to be delineated. Background, too, can be gouged out in directional strokes around an object much like ripples around a pebble tossed in a stream. The students should be cautioned not to cut too deeply into the linoleum because the low ridges remaining can produce a unique textural effect. If students have difficulty with cutting because the linoleum is too hard, heat the linoleum by placing it on a cookie tin over an electric hot plate turned on to low heat.

In large classes and in situations in which materials are limited, proofs of the blocks in process can be obtained in an economical, effective manner by placing a sheet of newsprint over the cut-out block and with the side of a black crayon or oil pastel rub over the paper with a steady and even pressure. The resulting proof can furnish youngsters with clues to their progress.

Either water- or oil-base printing inks may be used for the final prints. Oil ink is generally recommended for best results, but water-soluble ink is suggested for crowded elementary school situations where expeditious cleanup is a vital factor. The ink may be rolled out with a rubber brayer on a discarded cookie tin or serving tray, a piece of tempered Masonite, or a commercially available inking platen. When the ink feels tacky, it is applied to the linoleum block.

There are a number of ways to take or "pull" a print. The youngsters may place the paper carefully on the inked block which has been removed to a clean area protected by newspapers. They apply strong and even pressure with a brayer, the heel of a metal tablespoon, or a commercial *baren*. Pull the paper off the lino block carefully. If water-soluble ink is used, this step must be speeded up because the ink dries swiftly and the paper may adhere. A commercial block-printing press is a welcome asset in printmaking when the school budget provides for it. A final hint: A supply of Bandaids is recommended.

CLAY

Every child in elementary school should have the opportunity to create and express his ideas in clay. Clay is malleable, flexible, pliable, unpredictable, resisting, and on occasion messy. Some youngsters respond to clay more enthusiastically than others but all children can benefit from the unique challenge of this earthy material.

Very young children in the primary grades are natural clay manipulators. They need very little encouragement as they poke, squeeze, pound, stretch, roll, and pinch the moist clay. They enjoy exploring all its possibilities.

No two youngsters will tackle clay modeling in the same manner. Some may pull out shapes from a ball or lump of clay; some may add pieces to the basic form. Some may begin a figure with the main body structure; others may start with appendages and head.

The teacher's main responsibility at this early stage is to provide the children with an adequate supply of workable clay. A ball of clay the size of a grapefruit is recommended for each child. Use newspapers or plastic sheeting for the protection of desk or table tops and introduce just enough stimulating motivation to get the youngster started.

A period of exploration and experimentation with the clay should precede every clay project. This is especially true in the upper grades. Youngsters need to get the feel of the clay before they can express a particular idea. During this orientation session, the teacher might call their attention to the desired plasticity of the clay, the necessity of keeping excess clay moist by rolling the crumbs into a single ball, and the mechanics of clay cleanup.

One way to introduce young children to the feel and the potential of clay is to initiate the "clay in a paper sack game." Give each child a ball of clay about the size of a grapefruit or orange and a paper sack. Tell them to put the clay in the sack and without looking inside, manipulate the clay in the bag until they feel they have made an interesting shape. Ask them to think with their hands. Encourage them to stretch the clay, pull on it, pinch it, squeeze it, and poke it with their fingers. Above all they must not peek inside the bag until they have completed the manipulation. The finished pieces may be displayed on the desks or counters for all the students to see. Ask the youngsters in what way are the clay forms the same? How are they different? Does anyone see the form of an animal, bird, or fish in the clay? What did they learn about clay?

The animal kingdom provides a wealth of inspiration for the young artist. Four-legged mammals such as cows, horses, elephants, hippos, and bears are especially recommended because the child can make them stand up with ease. Other popular animals to model in clay are cats, dogs, rabbits, snakes, turtles, squirrels, and alligators. Group projects with themes such as *Noah's Ark*, *Three-Ring Circus*, *The Zoo*, *The Farm*, and *The Jungle* are very popular with young children. Human figures are a little more difficult for them to master, unless the child is guided to provide additional supports or construct thick, sturdy legs that will hold the figure in balance.

Primary school children are especially interested in the mobility and adaptability of clay. They may tell a whole story with one figure, such as a clown, manipulating it to create various postures. Their clown might stand on his head, bend backwards, or fall down. For young children clay may fulfill a definite therapeutic and story-telling need.

Some technical assistance may have to be given the young children who experience difficulty with their clay construction. For youngsters who have a tendency to pat their clay into a flat cookie shape, suggest that they cup the ball of clay in their hands as they form the body of the animal, bird, or fish they are making. In this way they will have more success in achieving a three-dimensional sculpture. Once they have modeled the characteristic shape of the animal, they can pull out or add arms, legs, tails, trunks, horns, and tusks.

The teacher might suggest a simple way to make the appendages adhere strongly to the main body by

A clay baby hippo shown in three stages. Top: Basic body with legs added. A tongue depressor may be used to make the mouth opening. Center: Addition of characteristic details: ears, eyes, teeth. Note the plastic quality of the clay is retained to give the animal authenticity. Discourage the smoothing out of clay surfaces with an excess of water.

inserting them into holes made in the clay with the fingers. For children in the upper grades, the process of scoring and welding clay can be demonstrated and explained. To counteract a sagging form, supplementary clay supports such as a fifth leg under the animal's body can be suggested. When the clay is leather-hard, this support can be removed. At all times the teacher should emphasize the importance of working toward a simple, sturdy, yet characteristic interpretation.

Though many children in the primary grades are not concerned with details as such, there will always be a number who find excitement in experimenting with textures and patterned relief on their clay creations. A collection of found objects such as popsicle sticks, bottle caps, nails, screws, plastic forks and spoons, buttons, shells, nuts, bark, beads, round wood clothespins, wrapping cord, combs, toothbrushes, and pieces of wire mesh will spark interest in decorative possibilities. All found objects should be washed and dried thoroughly after each use.

When youngsters reach the third and fourth grades, they are often more successful in mastering the challenging complexities of advanced clay modeling. However, they may ask for specific help with the problems of figures and appendages that sag or come

These Gaudi-like clay constructions, hinting perhaps at fantastic sea castles, are the imaginative expressions of young Japanese children. Clay is a popular and widely employed art medium in all Japanese elementary schools.

apart, balance and proportion, intricate delineation, and features such as eyes, mouths, ears, beaks, snouts, and horns.

At this stage a number of effective motivations may be included in the teaching repertoire: field trips to observe and sketch animals at a farm, ranch, zoo, animal shelter, or natural museum; family pets brought to class as models; photographs of animals; films of animals in their habitats; and large reproductions of drawings, paintings, and sculptures of animals by artists of many countries. If the project involves making pottery, a visit to a college ceramics department or to a contemporary potter's studio will whet student interest and provide authoritative answers to pertinent questions.

As a subject for clay sculpture, the prehistoric dinosaur fires the imagination of children, especially of those youngsters who are developing a strong interest in natural science and in the wonders of the universe. The theme of earth's primeval giants intrigues children. Perhaps they have read that the bones of some prehistoric monster have been found in their own state. They may even have seen colossal, reconstructed skeletons in a museum of natural history. The dinosaur, indeed, is uniquely adapted to interpretation in clay—the characteristic mass of the creature, ponderous, monumental, armorlike, its rough, eroded, wrinkled skin evoking the quality of the elemental earth itself.

A preliminary drawing for clay projects in the upper grades is optional. Quite often, however, it helps youngsters clarify their visual concept of the animal or figure they plan to model. For a clay dinosaur

A 14-inch high pot by a fifth grader who used the double-pinch pot technique. Two pinch pots are joined together, then paddled with a cord-wrapped paddle into a more varied shape. Foot and neck are added when the clay has set slightly. Detail shows the rich texture achieved by using clay slabs, pellets, and impressions made into the clay with found objects.

project the teacher may have to allot a greater amount of clay to each student than suggested for primary grade clay activities. In any case, extra prepared clay should always be ready for emergencies.

For those students who need help in undertaking their clay dinosaur, a fundamental body structure based on the post and lintel technique is suggested. A lump of clay slightly larger than a grapefruit is rolled out into a thick, heavy coil to form the body, tail, neck, and sometimes head of the dinosaur. For the legs, four or more rolled coils of clay are attached securely to the body. Make holes in the body structure with a finger and push the appendages into them, then strengthen the junctures with additional clay. In order to prevent uneven shrinkage or cracking when firing the clay, armature supports such as wire, sticks, twigs, or reed should not be used inside the structure.

Planned preliminary discussions by students and teacher should center on the structural possibilities that can give character to the dinosaur—the sway of the body, stance and counterstance of the legs, swing of the tail, turn of the head, action of jaws, and flare of wings. In some instances an imaginatively expressive dinosaur may combine the characteristics of a number of different prehistoric monsters. At all stages during the modeling, the clay animal should be viewed from every angle so that the youngster can develop the form as three-dimensionally as possible. A 12-inch square Masonite working base for the clay will help make this possible.

There are almost no limits to clay relief and textural exploitation where older children are involved.

Youngsters employ found objects such as buttons, clothespins, bottle caps, bark, wire mesh, shells, nuts, and bolts to add texture and pattern to clay creations.

Whether their creation is a clay pot, figure, animal, or clay relief, the field of decoration is wide open. The found object collection will provide a welcome source of texture-making tools. To achieve the scaly and armorlike skin of certain dinosaurs, students might roll out balls, coils, and ribbons of clay and apply them to the main body of the animal. Slip (water-diluted clay) can be used as an adhesive to secure the pellets or strips of clay. Discarded broken saw blades, pencils, beads, plastic forks, cord, natural objects such as bark, coral, shells, nuts, weeds, and assorted hardware can be used to incise and impress unique textural effects.

If a kiln is available and the animals are to be fired, they should be allowed to dry evenly and slowly until leather-hard. They may be stored to dry in a cabinet or on a counter under a sheet of plastic. In the case of large animals, holes or hollows should be made in their understructures while the piece is still leather-hard. These apertures allow the moisture to escape and prevent cracking or exploding of the clay during the firing.

Kiln glazing of the fired clay pieces is rarely undertaken in the elementary school because of limited budgets and firing facilities. However, there are other avenues to the enrichment of bisque or fired clay. Among these, staining is definitely recommended for projects in the upper grades. Shoe polish, wood stains, oil pastel or powder paint rubbed into the clay, colored tissue paper applied with white glue, moist dirt, Rub'n'Buff, and Treasure Gold are among the possibilities for applying a finish or patina to the bisque ware.

PLASTER RELIEF

Youngsters in the upper grades are often self-critical concerning their drawing ability and need the satisfaction and challenge of creating in an art medium not always dependent on drawing or painting skills. Techniques involving manipulative materials and special tools whet their expressive appetites, and even though a preliminary sketch is usually recommended, the fact that it can be freely interpreted and changed in the ensuing process often ensures their enthusiastic approval.

Art projects that belong in this category are lino prints, collographs, metal repoussé, ceramics, subtractive sculpture, papier-mâché, stitchery, weaving, and constructions involving found objects. A popular project that youngsters respond to, and have much success with, is the plaster relief.

For a relief sculpture in this medium the following materials and tools are recommended: moist earth

Subject themes for plaster reliefs are found everywhere. Here "Animals of the Jungle" provided the motivational impetus for the top and center illustrations. The Bible story "Jonah and the Whale" inspired the interpretation in the bottom relief.

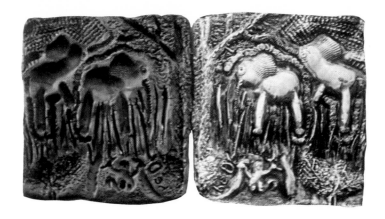

clay; plaster; a plastic or rubber dishpan; a container for the clay mold (shoe box, cigar box, half-gallon or gallon milk carton); an assortment of discarded or found objects of all kinds—spools, nails, wire lath, screws, keys, bottle caps, buckles, round wooden clothespins, rope, cord, beads, reed, plastic forks and spoons, as well as natural objects such as twigs, pine cones, acorns, nuts, seashells and bark; a plaster-sealing medium such as white glue or shellac; a small utility brush; and staining liquids (wood stains, diluted oil paints, commercial patina pastes).

The first step in the project is to prepare the box for the clay mold. In the case of a shoebox, simply reinforce the box with a strip of masking tape around the top edge. Put the lid under the box to reinforce that area. The inside of the box may be sealed with melted paraffin or lined with wax paper. If a milk carton is used, cut it in half lengthwise. If the open end is resealed with tape, both halves of the carton may be used. No protective coat is needed. In the case of the cigar box, remove lid and seal the interior with paraffin or wax paper.

Two methods of making the basic clay layer are suggested. In the simplest procedure the clay is rolled out in a slab approximately ½ to 1 inch thick, cut to the size of the box, and placed in the bottom of the box ready for the next stage. In the second method, the clay is placed in the bottom of the box, pellet by pellet, until the bottom is filled to a depth of ½ to 1 inch. If a very flat clay surface is desired, the clay may be stamped with the end of a wood block.

Before the students begin their impressions in the clay mold, they should practice designs on a small slab of clay using various imprinting tools. Discussion and demonstration should reveal that an impression made in the clay will be the reverse in the plaster cast. Designs pressed in will bulge out. Letters, numbers, and names must be imprinted backwards in order to read correctly in the final product.

By building a clay wall around a student's practice clay piece and filling it with plaster, the teacher can make a quick cast to show the class what happens in the process. Knowing the limits and the possibilities of this exciting medium frees the student to be more innovative, more expressive.

There are a number of ways to build the clay negative mold. A very free and natural approach may involve the use of hands and fingers. Commercial ceramic tools may also be employed. Coils, pellets, and ribbons of clay cut out from a thin slab may be applied with slip.

With younger children it might be wise to limit the design or subject matter to those ideas that can be best expressed with the impressions of the found objects available. In this approach, instead of scratch-

---

The clay negative mold and the completed plaster relief are illustrated above. Note that because a reverse image results, letters and numerals must be impressed backwards into the clay mold to read correctly in the final relief. Shapes pressed into the clay bulge out in the plaster version. A seashell was employed for the elephant's ears. Other effective imprinting found objects include beads, clothespins, bottle caps, nuts, bark, crumpled heavy-duty aluminum foil, cork, heavy cord, reeds, and buttons.

ing or incising lines in the clay with a nail or stick, a procedure which produces sharp and troublesome edges in the final plaster cast, the children press their lines into the clay. For straight lines they may use reeds, applicator sticks, the edges of a popsickle stick, or the edge of a piece of cardboard. For curved lines they might use bent reed, cord, string, or bent wire. Children of all ages enjoy the variety of textures and pattern they can create through the combination of the various imprinting objects.

Recommended subject matter themes for plaster relief include imaginative birds, fish, insects, animals in their habitats, flower gardens, legendary or Biblical figures, heraldic devices, personal insignia, and non-object designs.

When the impressions are completed, liquid plaster mix is poured over the clay mold approximately ½ to 1 inch in thickness. Before the plaster sets, bent paper clips may be inserted into it to provide hanging hooks for the completed plaster relief. For a concise explanation on plaster-mixing procedures, see the following section "Sculpture." Allow sufficient time for the plaster to set. This may vary from 1 to 2 or more hours. Some teachers suggest letting the plaster dry overnight. It is recommended that the teacher make a sample plaster mold a day or so before the actual project to test the plaster.

When the plaster is hard, the student pries open the cardboard container or carton and separates the clay from the plaster. If this separation is handled

carefully, most of the moist clay in the mold can be saved for another project.

To prepare the plaster relief for the staining or glazing, the youngster should file, cut, or sandpaper the excess edges and sharp points that might be abrasive. The relief can then be washed with water. A discarded toothbrush can be used to clean the clay out of recessed areas. Before staining, give the plaster relief a generous coat of slightly water-diluted white glue or clear shellac. Let this coating dry thoroughly.

The most successful color stains for this project are wood stains, shoe stains, or oil paints generously diluted with turpentine. Oil colors recommended are raw umber, burnt umber, raw sienna, burnt sienna, ochre, and earth green. If only bright colors are available, they should be neutralized or subdued with their complements. Apply the stains with a brush, let the paint flow into the indentations and incisions, then wipe off the surface as desired with paper towel or cloth to bring out highlights. For further embellishment try the Rub'n'Buff and Treasure Gold patinas in gold, silver, and pastel colors.

For situations in which color staining of the reliefs is not possible, the dry plaster may be tinted by mixing it with powder paints before sifting it into the water and pouring the cast.

Plaster reliefs might just be the answer for elementary school teachers and their students who are looking for exciting, challenging art projects. For many students this project will remind them of the sand sculptures created at beaches.

Steps in making a plaster relief employing a discarded aluminum pie container for the clay mold. Primary grade children are quite successful in this project and happy with the results. It is recommended that the youngsters press their designs into the clay rather than dig them out to ensure that the mold separates successfully.

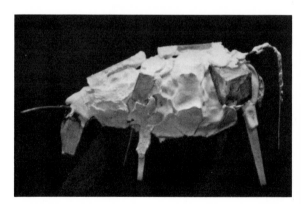

SCULPTURE

Subtractive sculpture in semihard materials can prove an exciting and rewarding art technique for upper-grade children if it is introduced as a serious and aesthetic challenge. Too often sculpture in the elementary school has been presented as a therapeutic activity with minor emphasis on its expressive potential.

If sufficient time cannot be allotted in the schedule for the youngsters to become thoroughly involved in the sculptural process, then it should be postponed until the middle school years. However, if the teacher understands some of the possibilities and the limitations of the sculptural medium and the students are sufficiently motivated to tackle the technique and carry it to its rewarding culmination, the experience can be one of the most fulfilling in the art program.

Recommended and readily obtainable materials for subtractive sculpture projects include molding plaster, clay, and lightweight firebrick. Commercially available products specifically recommended for carving include Featherrock, Crea-stone, and Foamglass.

Subject ideas for sculpture that youngsters can handle quite successfully include fish, birds, animals (especially those in repose), portraits or imaginary heads, organic and nonobjective free-forms including motifs based on rocks, shells, nuts, and other natural or biomorphic inspiration.

If plaster is selected as the medium, it should be mixed with additives such as fine grain zonolite or sand to give it texture and make it easier to carve. One part additive to one part of plaster will produce a fairly porous and workable block. A half-gallon or

Sculpture in the elementary school may include a variety of materials: plaster cast, sandcore, wood, wire, papier-mâché, porous firebrick, soap, and paraffin. It is essential, however, that sufficient time be allotted for the students to become thoroughly involved in the sculpture process. Facing page: Steps in an applied plaster sculpture show the basic armature of pliable wire and wood sticks. Newspaper may be used for stuffing and bulk. In plaster projects such as this, mix only a small amount of plaster at a time. Keep lots of newspapers on hand for protection of work areas. Never pour excess plaster down the sink!

quart size waxed-paper milk carton makes an adequate container for the plaster mold.

While the students are making preliminary sketches (optional) of their sculpture, the teacher can supervise two or more students at a time in the making of plaster molds. At a newspaper-covered table or counter near the sink, if possible, all the necessary materials should be available: plaster, zonolite or sand, scoops or cups, wax milk cartons opened wide at top, water, rubber or pliable plastic dishpan, wood stick, and dry tempera colors (if desired). Newspapers should cover the floor around the mixing area and line the wastebasket near at hand.

Fill milk carton three-quarters full with water. Pour this water into dishpan. Sift plaster into water slowly using hand, cup, or scoop. When islands of plaster appear above the water, add zonolite or sand. Stir gently yet swiftly with hand, squeezing the lumps until thoroughly mixed. The mixture thickens very quickly, so be ready to pour immediately into milk carton. Tap plaster-filled carton on the table to remove trapped air bubbles or stir quickly with a long stick or wooden spatula. Excess plaster left in dishpan should be scraped into a newspaper-lined wastebasket. *Never pour plaster down the sink!* Let the plaster mold harden completely. This may take several hours. In most instances teachers allow it to dry overnight. If color is desired in the plaster mold, dry tempera colors may be used to tint the dry plaster before it is mixed with water. Colors such as umber, ochre, sienna, and dull green are recommended.

The students may transfer their sketches to the

Three different finishes for plaster sculpture. In all instances plaster was combined with fine Zonolite to make the block easier to carve. Top: Completed carving coated with white glue, then painted with walnut stain. Bottom: Sealed with white glue, then coated with Sculpmetal, painted with India ink, and burnished with steel wool when dry.

Kububuwakota (Cape Dorset) Hunter. Soapstone. 25" Collection Aberbach Fine Art Gallery, New York City. The lives of Eskimo carvers are influenced greatly by the fortunes of hunting, so we see in their art a keen observation of game and the special characteristics of the hunt. How simple yet how beautiful their interpretations are! They know instinctively what is essential, what is superfluous in their work. A noted sculptor was once asked how he created his renowned horses. His answer: "I carve away everything that doesn't look like a horse."

plaster block with carbon paper or draw directly on the block with pencil. They may prefer to carve directly using their sketch as a reference only. If they use a sketch, they cut, file, rasp, or chisel away the excess plaster to delineate a profile view. Next they may use their top, front, and rear sketches and cut into their blocks to define those contours. They should proceed slowly and cautiously as they remove the excess plaster. The best tools for this process are the Sloyd or Hyde knife with the 2-inch semisharp blade or a small open plaster rasp. At this stage the youngsters should keep turning their sculpture pieces around to define the forms consistently. Working areas should be covered with newspapers to expedite cleanup. One teacher solved the messy problem by having the youngsters hold the plaster mold inside a cardboard grocery carton as they cut away the excess.

The teacher should help the students evaluate their work in process; to be aware of large shapes contrasting against small shapes, to see that one form flows gracefully into another, to capture the characteristic gesture or action, to emphasize a significant feature

such as the beak or claws of a bird, the gill of a fish, or the horns of a bull, and to enrich the surface through textures and pattern used sensitively and economically.

Nails, discarded dental tools, and nut picks are very effective for incising lines and descriptive detail. When the carving and delineation are complete, the sculpture may be stained, glazed, antiqued, or waxed if desired. To provide a working surface for the stain or patina, the plaster piece should be coated or sealed with an application of shellac or water-diluted white liquid glue. Allow this coating to dry thoroughly.

Perhaps the simplest method of staining the piece is to apply one of the many wood stains available. These come in a variety of subtle colors including a new dark earth green. Apply the stain freely with a brush and let it penetrate into the incised or textured areas of the plaster. Allow this to set briefly and then wipe off raised areas with a cloth to bring out highlights. If stain did not penetrate incised designs, reincise those areas and stain again. Tube oil paints diluted with turpentine to a liquid consistency may also be used as staining agents.

A study of sculpture through the ages tells us that the most honest and direct approach in carving is best. Primitive peoples sculpted a variety of arts and artifacts to use in their everyday life. Form followed function naturally and beautifully. The African

equestrian figure carved in wood, above, is an example of the honesty, integrity, restraint, and understatement that timeless sculpture evokes. Collection of Mr. and Mrs. Chet LaMore, Ann Arbor, Michigan.

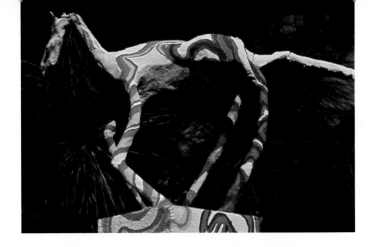

PAPIER-MÂCHÉ TECHNIQUES

*Children in the upper grades usually possess the necessary
technical and manipulative skills that the papier-mâché process
demands. The teacher should have all the required tools and
materials for the project organized beforehand: newspapers,
string, wire, tape, wheat paste, plastic containers, liquid laundry
starch, tempera paint, colored tissue paper, yarn, scissors, wire
cutters, wood bases, found objects, and whatever else is needed.
Storage for papier-mâché projects in process must also be
planned. Some techniques a teacher might present, depending
on class size, time allotted, materials available, and theme
selected are: (1). A basic framework of rolled newspapers
secured with string or masking tape (see below). (2). A wood or
wire armature. (3). A chicken- or screen wire-mesh armature
when group projects lead to massive forms. In the illustrations,
right, by interning classroom teachers, the students drilled holes
in a wood base and secured their wire and newspaper armature
into these holes making the ensuing construction much easier to
manage. Note the effectively coordinated painted designs on
both base and sculpture. Photos courtesy Oliver Coleman,
University of Georgia, Athens.*

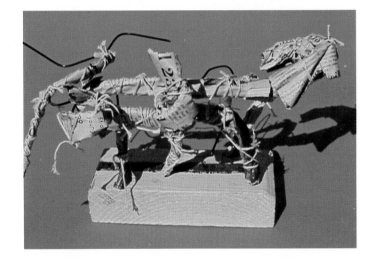

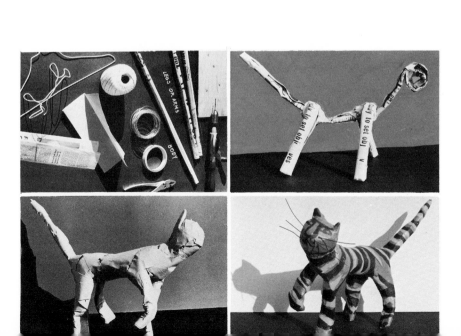

CONSTRUCTIONS IN SPACE

A whole new world of additive sculpture has opened up with the growing utilization of materials such as reeds, drinking straws, pick-up sticks, paste sticks, applicator sticks, assorted toothpicks, found materials, fast-drying glues, and metal adhesives. Whatever one may label the resulting constructions, whether space modulators, stabiles, mobiles, or assemblages, they definitely attract and hold the interest of today's space-conscious youngster and add a new, exciting dimension to the elementary art program.

The teacher's first consideration in the implementation of these construction projects is to see that sufficient materials and tools are on hand. Adequate storage facilities for constructions in progress must also be planned. A letter to the parents, including a list of found materials especially useful in three-dimensional constructions, might help build a store of

Facing page: Photograph by Dr. W. Robert Nix, University of Georgia, Athens. This page, top: Construction employing reed and construction paper. Grade 5; Bottom: Space modulator created with paper strips. Grade 6. Milwaukee.

discards and scraps that would get the project started (see Appendix E for suggestions).

In many instances the children will want to create nonobjective, abstract, or geometrically oriented constructions allowing the materials to dictate the form. This is particularly true when straws, applicator sticks, toothpicks, or reeds are the medium. The design grows, stick by stick, straw by straw, pick by pick, reed by reed.

Unless the construction itself has a stable footing, it is advisable that an auxiliary base of wood, or plywood be utilized. A painted cigar box makes a satisfactory base. If necessary, it can be weighted with sand and sealed with tape to stabilize it. Determine the number and the placement of the supports required, then drill or punch small holes into the base at these points. Begin the structure by inserting and gluing the initial reeds, sticks, toothpicks, or straws into these holes. The number of these supports or underpinnings will vary depending on the complexity and size of the structure.

The students and teacher will discover, too, a host of affinitive materials to enrich or embellish the stick and reed constructions. Many of these may be found objects such as bottle corks, thread spools, wood clothes pins, balsa wood strips, string, wood beads, pegs and buttons, round fishing corks, Ping Pong balls, pegboard scraps, small rubber balls, colored tissue and construction paper, plastic scraps, and cardboard rings from Scotch tape dispensers.

The completed constructions may be given a coat of spray paint if desired. Black or white is especially effective in unifying different parts of the structure

---

Wood scraps, tattered rope, straw, dried corn husks, discarded metal screen, and spools from thread or yarn can be exploited effectively in today's school art programs as these illustrations prove. Let the child's imagination soar!

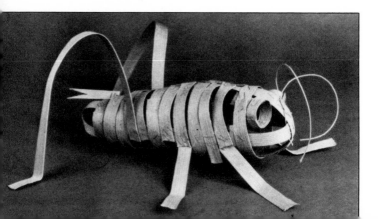

and creating a strong, visual impact. Always apply paint in a well-ventilated area.

There are many avenues open to the youngster who wishes to explore the possibilities of constructive or additive sculpture. Wire sculpture has a special appeal to boys. Wire can be combined with found metal objects to create exciting three-dimensional inventions. Toothpick and applicator stick constructions can be coated with or dipped into melted crayon or wet plaster. Corrugated cardboard can be cut into various-sized shapes then slotted and glued together into a stabile. Cardboard mailing tubes can be cut into various-sized cylinders and circles, then assembled into animals, insects, and figures. It is recommended that a vibrating jig saw (Dremel) be used to cut heavy cardboard or cardboard tubes.

BOX SCULPTURE

Older children often need a change of pace sparked by new challenges, materials, and techniques to keep them interested in art. Imaginative constructions utilizing cardboard boxes, mailing tubes, and assorted found objects give upper-grade youngsters a rare opportunity to express their individual ideas in a unique three-dimensional form, recycle discarded materials into new configurations, struggle with a problem of intricate construction until it is resolved, and prove once more the old adage that "the whole is greater than the sum of its parts" in a truly creative way.

At least 2 to 3 weeks before the project begins, the children should be reminded to start collecting discarded boxes of all sizes and shapes from grocery, stationery, drug, shoe, and department stores. This early personal involvement on the part of the youngsters builds high interest in the adventure ahead.

All the accumulated boxes and found objects can be stored until needed in a large cardboard carton or, if desired, each child could keep his or her own collection of items in a strong paper shopping bag labeled with the child's name.

Tools, equipment, and special materials that can contribute to the success of the project include straight pins, masking tape, paper clips, string, double-faced tape, rubber bands, gum tape, coping saw, vibrating jig saw (optional), white liquid glue, rubber cement, school paste, scissors, paper punch, nails, wire, old magazines, and coloring materials. X-acto knives and single-edge razor blades (preferably in holders or safely taped) are essential for cutting holes in the cardboard boxes but they must be handled with caution under strict teacher supervision and guidance.

Several problems unique to this project should be resolved before the class begins the actual box constructions. These include adequate storage for the found objects and for the constructions in progress as well as a sufficient supply of fastening equipment and materials.

Imaginative themes for box constructions are almost limitless: spacemen, space stations and ships, robots, creatures from another planet, toys, rockets, homes and vehicles of the future, fantastic designs for playground equipment, and nonobjective space modulators.

One method of initiating the project is to ask the children to select three or four different-sized boxes and tubes from the general supply or from their individual collections and manipulate these into vari-

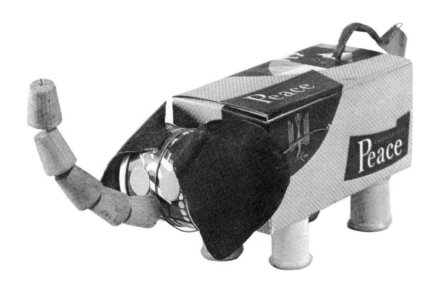

Let the shape of the box itself trigger the student's imagination. Square and rectangular boxes, which were used for the ship sculpture above, are much easier for young children to assemble. It is not always necessary to paint box sculpture. The elephant, right, has a trunk made of corks.

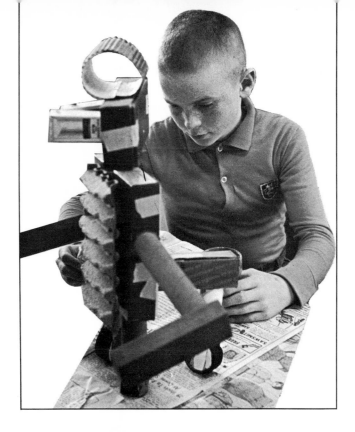

ous juxtapositions until some arrangement or structure triggers a subject idea. After the youngsters decide on the basic shape of their creation, they may want to make some sketches to help them with their construction, although such drawings are optional. The real excitement builds as the youngster sees the construction grow and change as new materials are found and added. What began conceptually as a *Dream Car* might easily emerge in the final stages as *A Creature from Another Planet*.

The most difficult part of this project is the mechanics involved in fastening the separate boxes together and securing the appendages to the main structure. Some recommended approaches are: Glue, then tie the boxes together with string or cord until the glue dries; fasten the glued boxes together with a ribbon of masking tape that goes around both boxes; in many instances the glue should be allowed to dry overnight for a strong weld.

In the construction of standing monsters, spacemen, or other fantastic creatures, the problem of making the figure stand upright must be resolved. If necessary, a third leg or support should be created. Sometimes a tail can be added for balance, sometimes the arms can hold gear that touches the ground for a stabilizer.

Interest in the project may be renewed by suggesting further implementation with other found materials for textural or decorative delineation. Encourage the children to exploit egg cartons, corrugated cardboard, paper drinking straws, plastic packing noodles, round wooden clothespins, plain and colored toothpicks, paste sticks, dowel rods, corks, pipe

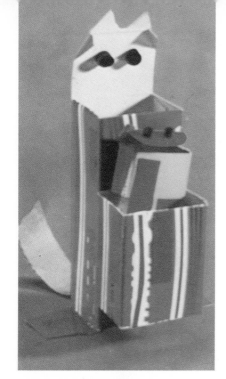

cleaners, wooden beads, Ping Pong balls, and game pieces. Some of these materials may be purchased in quantities at little cost from discount houses or school supply firms.

The outcome of this project depends in great part on the number and variety of boxes and other found items gathered by students and teacher. Sometimes an unusual box turns up that is just right for the head of a monster and provides the inspiration for the rest of the construction. Often a box can be partially opened and hinged to become the mouth and jaws of a voracious animal.

Top left: *Plastic containers in all sizes may be recycled into odd, fantastic creatures. Care must be exercised when cutting into plastic. It may be prudent to reserve such constructions for upper grade children.* Top right: *Note how the box lids in the sculpture become the heads of the mother and baby kangaroo.*

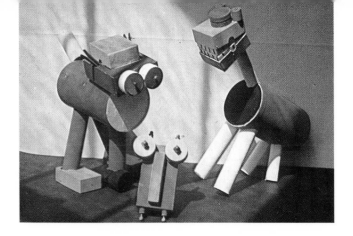

A decision must be made, too, on whether to paint the box construction or not. In some instances, the basic containers with their printed designs are so colorful and exciting that painting them would only detract from their expressive and unique quality. However, in cases in which the sculpture is not painted, the characteristic features that give the creature or figure its individuality must be emphasized, especially the eyes, ears, nose, and mouth.

If the constructions are to be painted, certain factors will have to be taken into consideration. The glossy surfaces of many boxes will resist tempera or watercolor paints. Soap will have to be added to paint to make it adhere. Latex paint or enamel covers all surfaces effectively. If cost is not a factor, spray paint is recommended. Perhaps copper, silver or gold could be used for a robot or spaceman. Apply in a well-ventilated area or out of doors.

Another possibility is to cover or mask the distracting parts of the boxes by camouflaging them with a collage treatment of colored construction paper, newspaper, comic book sheets, colored tissue paper, magazine cutouts, wallpaper samples, or discarded decorative wrapping and gift papers.

There are endlessly exciting possibilities in box and found object sculpture. The teacher and students who are resourceful enough, curious enough, and persistent enough to try this project have a real "adventure in art" awaiting them.

A plastic container was combined with other plastic discards to produce the imaginatively fantastic robot illustrated on this page. The entire construction was sprayed with metal paint. When spraying sculpture, do it out of doors or in a well-ventilated area. Always protect working surfaces with newspapers. Grade 6, Ann Arbor, Michigan.

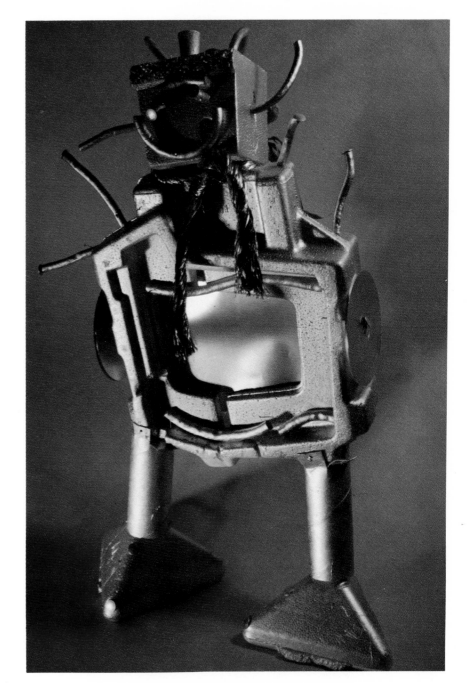

MASKS

Mask making in the elementary schools has always been a popular activity but unfortunately one in which the design considerations have seldom been fully understood or effectively implemented. Too often compositional factors involving the mask aesthetic have been minimized and colors applied in a random form-negating manner.

The most exciting and evocative masks of past centuries have almost always been based on an abstract, stylized concept rather than on natural appearances, and often on a format that utilized symbolic and simple shapes such as the oval, circle, ellipse, or a combination of these. Masks of various ethnological and primitive cultures often owe their impact to a semisymmetrical version of the face, whether of man or animal.

Although very young children can, on occasion, create colorful, expressively naive masks if effectively

Colored construction paper masks with three-dimensional effect achieved by cutting slits into the borders of a square or rectangular sheet of paper, then overlapping the resulting tabs and stapling them together. Masks make highly decorative motifs to brighten up the classroom.

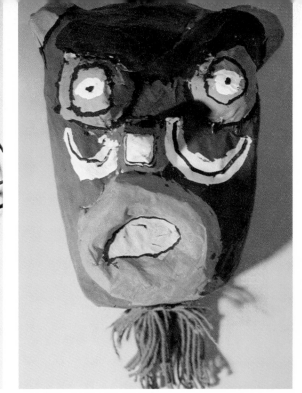

motivated, mask making, because of its symbolic connotations, traditional overtones, and often complex techniques, should usually be postponed until youngsters reach the upper elementary grades.

A study of masks by tribal Africans and North Pacific Coast Indians, among others, reveals certain significant and recurring aspects. Facial features that capture mood or spirit are emphasized or exaggerated. Characteristic elements of a face are seldom minimized or distorted to appear as something they are not, such as the trite asterisk-shaped eyes or mouth that are found in stereotyped versions.

The most impressive masks are imbued with the essence of a particular mood: astonishment, serenity, power, anger, dignity, reverence, joy, fury, peace, frenzy, despair, or wonder. A continuity of facial forms and features, as exemplified by the movement of the nose structure into the eyebrow contour, is a major characteristic in primitive masks.

Facial decoration can be effectively employed to heighten the visual quality of a mask. Students may use lines that repeat and emphasize dominant features, markings to create pattern or texture on the face, or lines that delineate the hair or beard. Eyes are usually emphasized by using highly contrasting colors or values. Color should be used judiciously since it can either enhance or jeopardize the mask's impact. It must be integrated with the features, not superficially applied, and must complement rather than negate the mask's dominant characteristics. Subtle

Illustrated are varied approaches to mask making. Left: Boxes, spools, paper cups, and yarn were employed. Center: Construction paper and raffia. Feathers may also be incorporated. Right:

Papier-mâché applied over a crumpled paper base. Mask forms can also be constructed by applying newspaper strips over a mixing bowl with wheat paste or liquid starch.

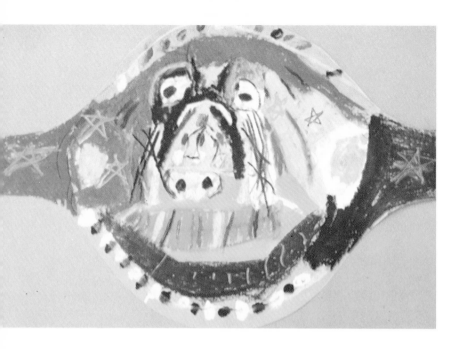

Left: *Mask designed in oil pastel on colored construction paper by first grade child.* Right: *Kindergarten children designed their own Halloween costumes using paper sacks from cleaning* establishments. *If these are unavailable, secure two giant grocery bags together.*

and limited color schemes and combinations should be encouraged. The primary colors should be used with discretion, although they may be effectively employed to provide necessary contrast.

The incentive for mask making may spring just as naturally from social studies or literature lessons as it does from overworked Halloween themes. Children should be challenged to create masks as art forms per se.

Materials and processes that lead to qualitative mask making are in a sense limited. Papier-mâché over a clay base or mold is still the most effectively controlled technique allowing for highly individual interpretations and for delicate facial modeling. Also recommended is papier-mâché or plaster-impregnated gauze applied over a found object or kitchen utensil such as a mixing bowl, round plastic dishpan or salad bowl, balloon, or beach ball. As the form develops it can be embellished with additional pieces of Styrofoam, bent cardboard, and found objects to create nose, eye, mouth, and ear shapes and with string, yarn, or raffia for hair, beard, and

other textures. These details are covered with a final layer of gauze or paper toweling and then the entire mask is painted if desired.

A popular mask-making technique is the paper sculpture method, but it generally requires intricate cutting and scoring of paper to achieve effective three-dimensional features. It has many possibilities, however, and can be pursued in the ordinary classroom because of the availability of materials and tools. It is recommended that a period of exploration be scheduled to discover the three-dimensional potential of paper before embarking on the mask project itself.

For children in the primary grades the creation of a paper plate, paper sack, or totem style mask is the most practical approach since it does not involve a complex three-dimensional technique.

A study of early Pacific Coast Indian life provides rich motivation for many art projects, including the construction of a totem pole by the class as a whole. To begin with, let the children choose a sheet of 12 × 18 inch colored construction paper as the background for their totem masks. Placing the paper horizontally on their desks, 18 inch border at the bottom, they draw their mask with white chalk in the center of the paper. The larger they draw it the better. The top and bottom of their masks can touch the paper's edge if they wish. Following the custom of the Indian totem carvers, they can make their masks represent an animal, bird, man, spirit, or whatever they desire.

When they complete their drawings, they may color their mask in several ways: they can paint it with

tempera; paste colored paper or cloth over it; or color it with crayon or oil pastels. They should be encouraged to exploit unusual colors in their mask, repeat colors for unity, create contrast by juxtaposing light and dark colors, and make important parts of the mask dominant through use of vivid colors.

When the mask is completed, parts of it may be made three-dimensional by cutting slits with a single-edged razor blade around an eye, nose, mouth, or ear and folding these outward from the main mask. A backing sheet of contrasting color is sometimes recommended. Youngsters may also add supplemental pieces for teeth, fangs, horns, earings, and eyebrows.

There are several methods of making totem poles out of the construction-paper masks. A recommended technique is to begin with an empty gallon tin food container from the cafeteria. Weight it with sand. Wrap a large sheet of plain or colored tagboard around it, fastening the sheet securely into a cylinder with a strong filament tape. Apply glue where the paper overlaps. Build another tagboard cylinder above the first if desired. Repeat until the height needed is reached. With the tagboard cylinder as a sturdy base, fasten the masks around it with glue, stapler, masking tape, or gun tacker. Once the basic totem is constructed, the youngsters may embellish it with additional wings, feet, and arms made out of painted cardboard. Display the completed totems in the school foyer for everyone to enjoy.

Masks designed for a totem pole project. 12" × 18" colored construction paper and oil pastels were the materials used. Completed masks were adhered to discarded food tins from the school cafeteria. Slits were cut in the mask and the paper folded out to create three-dimensional ears, teeth, noses, cheeks, and horns.

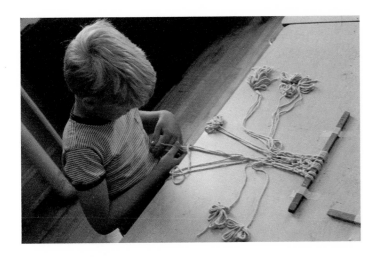

Illustrations on this page show children engaged in weaving and macramé projects. Recommended books on the teaching of weaving, stitchery, and related crafts are listed for the teacher in Appendix C.

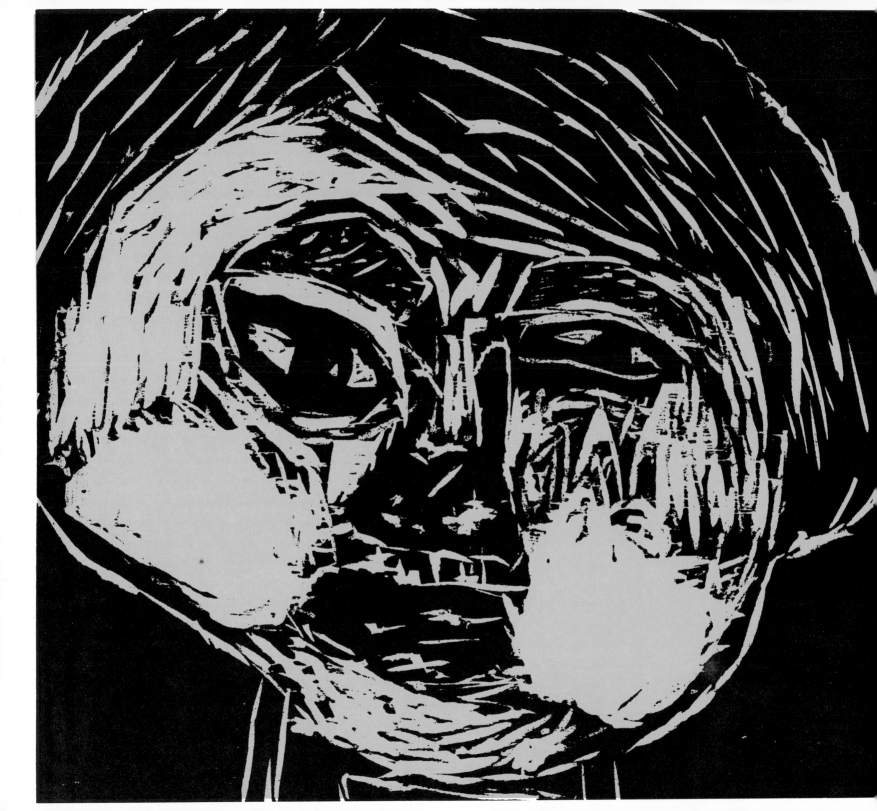

appendix

A

CHILDREN: THEIR CHARACTERISTICS

FIRST AND SECOND GRADERS (AGES FIVE, SIX, AND SEVEN)

Are rather active and easily excited
Like to work with their hands
Have a strong feeling of possessiveness
Are eager to learn
Want to be first
Have a limited span of interest
Are easily fatigued
Take great pride in their work
Are usually gregarious
Have feelings that are easily hurt
Are alternately cooperative and uncooperative
Can usually grasp only one idea at a time
Delight in imaginative games, stories, and plays

Facing page: *Woodblock print, Japan.* This page, top: *Linoleum print. Grade 3.* Bottom: *Children involved in painting are lost in a world of their own. Photo courtesy Naomi Dietz, Fullerton, California.*

Want the approval of classmates and teacher
Still live in their own secret world
Are interested in new things to touch and taste
Like to pretend and engage in make-believe
Are fascinated by moving and mechanical devices
Enjoy sports, television, holidays, illustrated books, family outings, school field trips, new clothes

THIRD AND FOURTH GRADERS (AGES SEVEN, EIGHT, AND NINE)

Have improved eye-hand coordination
Have better command of small muscles
Are becoming aware of differences in people
Begin to set standards for themselves
Are learning to be responsible, orderly, and cooperative
Begin to form separate sex groups
May join gangs or cliques
Enjoy comic books and magazines
Are growing in self-evaluation and evaluation of others
Are now able to concentrate for a longer period of time
Are developing a growing interest in travel
Are interested in the life processes of plants and animals
Are developing a sense of humor
Are avid hobbyists and collectors

The often traumatic experience of the first haircut is captured vividly and tearfully in this pen and ink drawing by a fourth grade child. How observant she is as she remembers that the sign reads backwards inside the beauty shop. Winona, Minnesota.

FIFTH AND SIXTH GRADERS
(AGES NINE, TEN, AND ELEVEN)

Are developing a set of values, a sense of right and wrong

Begin to concentrate more on individual interests

Are now more interested in activities that relate to their sex groupings

Are becoming more dependable, responsible, and reasonable

Are interested in doing things "right"

Develop interests outside of school—in their community and in the world itself

Begin to criticize grown-ups and anyone in authority

Are undergoing critical emotional and physical changes

Vary in maturity. Girls are often more developed physically, emotionally, physiologically, and mentally than boys

Build on their interest in collections and hobbies

Begin a phase of hero-worship

Very often like to be by themselves, away from adult interference

Are growing to be self-conscious and self-critical

Enjoy working in groups

Are developing an increasing interest-work span

Tend to form separate gangs or cliques according to hobbies, interests, sex, neighborhoods.

How much children really see when they are encouraged to be keen observers and noticers! The pattern of the bark in this tree gives it a life of its own. Osaka, Japan.

B

HOW CHILDREN GROW IN ART

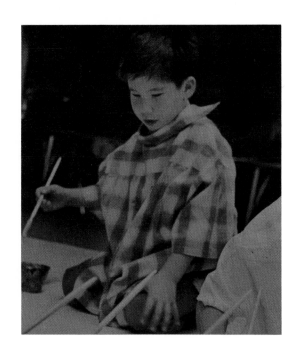

Knowing what young children are like and what their special interests and needs may be are important requisites for successful teaching but a basic understanding of what children do *naturally* in art as they draw and paint is just as necessary to the essential encouragement of their creative growth. The children's graphic potential and the richness and complexity of their imagery varies with the stages of their physical, mental, physiological, and sociological development. Some children may have had many preschool experiences in working with art materials; others may have had very limited creative opportunities. Some youngsters may have developed a keen interest in some particular phase of their environment, for example, in horses, cars, trains, bikes, birds, rockets, insects, and rock or shell collections;

thus their observations will often distinguish their art work from that of other children in the class because of its complexity, insight, and richness of detail. Since children express best what they know best and what they are most sensitive to, or affected by, it is often possible for the discerning teacher and parent to discover through their art what they respond most to in their environment and what their attitudes, values, and feelings about life may be.

FIRST GRADE CHILDREN (AGES FIVE AND SIX)

Continue to draw the geometrical symbols of the circle, square, triangle, oval, and rectangle together with the lines which they used earlier but now change and enrich these symbols as they react to new experiences.

Use a basic symbol, such as a circle, to depict varied, visual images—the sun, a human or animal head, a table, a flower, a tree top, even a room.

Devise many possible variations of a human figure, a house, a dog, a tree.

Repeat the symbols that they have mastered, over and over again.

Use combinations of symbols that are different from others in class.

Simplify their representations and are not too concerned with details.

Draw things as they know and feel them to be: the band of sky like a canopy at the top of the page, the sun that appears in the upper corner of almost every picture, the railroad tracks that do not converge, the eyes high in the head, the tree with a large trunk to make it strong.

Three-dimensional construction employing colored paper appeals to all children. They like to bend, fold, fringe and curl the paper, and cut out little doors and widows so they can peek into secret places. The "funny bunnies" were part of an Easter holiday project. The paper city is a group project by Japanese children.

Draw related objects such as house and tree on a base line which might be the bottom edge of the page or a line drawn horizontally above it.

Use color in a personal or emotional context without regard to its local use or identification.

SECOND GRADE CHILDREN (AGES SIX AND SEVEN)

Use color more naturalistically in some instances but as a rule limit themselves to one hue of green for all trees and leaves, one blue for the sky unless motivated to see more variety.

Change slowly, subtly from geometric, symbolic interpretations to more specific characterization and delineation.

Begin to use more details in their pictures—hair, ribbons, buttons, belt buckles, eyebrows, eye glasses, shoelaces, costume jewelry, fingernails, purses, patterns in clothes.

Sometimes draw both the inside and outside of a place, a person, or object in an x-ray interpretation.

May use a fold-over technique to show people on both sides of a street, people around a table or a swimming pool, or players on a baseball field. Often the youngsters turn their papers completely around as they draw.

Use characteristic apparel and detail to distinguish sexes, such as skirts and long hair for girls, trousers and shirts for boys.

Draw distant things the same size as those nearer them but place them higher on the page.

Sometimes draw things as they know them rather than how they see them, for example, a table with four legs when only two legs are visible, a house with three sides when only one side is visible.

The self-portraits left and on facing page are contour drawings by upper grade youngsters, Iowa City, Iowa. They reveal to us once again what children are capable of achieving in drawing skills when encouraged to be aware to notice characteristic features and details.

THIRD AND FOURTH GRADE CHILDREN (AGES SEVEN, EIGHT, AND NINE)

Begin to draw and compose with more conscious deliberate planning, striving for more realistic proportions.

Begin to create space and depth through use of overlapping shapes.

May now select and arrange objects to satisfy their compositional needs.

May in some instances introduce the horizon line to show distant space.

Now draw distant objects and figures smaller as well as higher on the page.

Make repeated efforts to show action in their drawings of people and animals but are often handicapped by their inability to master relative proportion and foreshortening.

FIFTH AND SIXTH GRADE CHILDREN (AGES NINE, TEN, AND ELEVEN)

Become increasingly critical of their drawing ability and often so discouraged with their efforts that they may lose interest in art class unless they are sympathetically guided, encouraged, and motivated.

Develop a growing curiosity to experiment with varied materials, tools, and complex processes.

Experiment with dark and light patterns, with neutralized colors, and with a variety of textural effects.

Begin to use rudimentary perspective principles in drawing landscapes, buildings, streets, sidewalks, train tracks, fences, and roads.

Choose subject matter for their art expression which relates to human interest and activities, community and world events, and current projects in ecology and space exploration.

Become more interested in their environment as a source for their drawings and paintings.

Sometimes attempt shading techniques to make drawn forms appear solid, cylindrical, and realistic.

Notice especially how the hair in the self-portraits here and on facing page is sensitively drawn, not just scribbled in as is so often the case. Observe, too, the careful delineation of the freckles, cracks in lips, eyes, eyelashes, and nostrils.

RECOMMENDED READINGS

BOOKS FOR CHILDREN

The letter following each book title indicates its suitability for (P) the primary grade child, (U) the upper grade child, (A) for children at all grade levels.

Baumann, Hans. 1954. *The Caves of the Great Hunters*. New York: Pantheon Books, Inc. (U)

Baylor, Byrd. 1972. *When Clay Sings*. New York: Charles Scribner's Sons. (U)

Borten, Helen. 1951. *Do You See What I See?* New York: Simon and Schuster, Inc. (P)

Broadatz, Phil. 1967. *Textures*. New York: Dover Publications, Inc. (U)

Browner, Richard. 1962. *Look Again!* New York: Atheneum Publishers. (P)

Busch, Phyllis S. 1968. *Lions in the Grass*. Cleveland: The World Publishing Co. (P)

Chase, Alice Elizabeth. 1962. *Famous Paintings*. New York: Platt and Munk. (U)

Deny, Norman and Filmer-Sankey, Josephine. 1966. *The Bayeux Tapestry*. New York: Atheneum Publishers. (U)

Fenton, Carrol L., and Fenton, Mildred E. 1963. *In Prehistoric Seas*. Garden City, N.Y.: Doubleday and Co., Inc. (A)

Fisher, James. 1957. *Wonderful World of the Sea*. New York: Garden City Books. (U)

Gill, Bob. 1963. *What Color is Your World?* New York: Ivan Abolensky, Inc. (A)

Gracza, Margaret. 1964. *The Ship and the Sea in Art*. Minneapolis: Lerner Publishing Co. (U)

———. 1965. *The Bird in Art*. Minneapolis: Lerner Publishing Co. (U)

Top: *Linoleum print. Grade 5. Teachers of the art class should bring these recommended books listed to the attention of the school librarian for possible purchase. Children who complete projects earlier than their classmates should be encouraged to become acquainted with books on art and artists. Always keep some books on art on hand in the classroom.*

Hammond, Penny, and Thomas, Katrina. 1963. *My Skyscraper City*. New York: Doubleday and Co., Inc. (A)

Harkoven, Helen B. 1964. *Circuses and Fairs*. Minneapolis: Lerner Publishing Co. (A)

Hay, John, and Strong, Arline. 1962. *A Sense of Nature*. Garden City, N.Y.: Doubleday and Co., Inc., (U)

Hellman, Harold. 1967. *Art and Science of Color*. New York: McGraw-Hill Book Co. (U)

Hoban, Tana. 1970. *Shapes and Things*. New York: The MacMillan Co. (A)

Janson, H. W., and Janson, D. J. 1963. *The Story of Painting for Young People*. New York: Harry N. Abrams, Inc. (U)

Kablo, Martin. 1963. *World of Color*. New York: McGraw-Hill Book Co. (P)

Katz, Herbert, and Katz, Marjorie. 1969. *Museum Adventures*. New York: Coward-McCann, Inc. (U)

Kessler, Leonard. 1958. *Art Is Everywhere*. New York: Dodd, Mead and Co. (U)

——. 1962. *The Worm, The Bird and You*. New York: Dodd, Mead and Co. (U)

——. 1961. *What's in a Line?* New York: William R. Scott, Inc. (A)

Kirn, Ann. 1959. *Full of Wonder*. New York: World Publishing Co. (A)

Krauss, Ruth. 1952. *A Hole Is to Dig*. New York: Harper and Row, Publishers. (P)

Law, Joseph. 1962. *Adam's Book of Odd Creatures*. New York: Atheneum Publishers. (A)

Lerner, Sharon. 1964. *The Self-Portrait in Art*. Minneapolis: Lerner Publishing Co. (U)

Lewis, Richard. 1966. *Miracles* (Poems by Children) New York: Simon and Schuster, Inc. (U)

Moore, Janet Gaylord. 1968. *The Many Ways of Seeing*. New York: World Publishing Co. (U)

Munari, Bruno. 1963. *Bruno Munari's Zoo*. New York: World Publishing Co. (P)

Munro, Eleanor C. 1961. *The Golden Encyclopedia of Art*. New York: Golden Press, Inc. (U)

Nickel, Helmut. 1969. *Warriors and Worthies*. New York: Atheneum Publishers. (U)

O'Neil, Mary. 1961. *Hailstones and Halibut Bones*. (Poems about colors) Garden City, N.Y.: Doubleday and Co., Inc. (A)

Paine, Roberta M. 1968. *Looking at Sculpture*. New York: Lothrop, Lee and Shepard Co., Inc. (U)

Piatti, Celestino. 1965. *The Happy Owls*. London: Ernest Benn Ltd. (A)

Provensen, Alice, 1967. *What is Color?* New York: Golden Press, Inc. (U)

Rieger, Shay. 1971. *Animals in Clay*. New York: Charles Scribner's Sons. (U)

Rockwell, Ann. 1968. *Glass, Stones and Crowns*. New York: Atheneum Press Inc. (U)

Ruskin, Ariane. 1964. *Story of Art for Young People*. New York: Pantheon Books, Inc. (U)

Scheele, E. Wilham. 1954. *Prehistoric Animals*. New York: World Publishing Co. (U)

Schlein, Miriam. 1958. *Shapes*. New York: William R. Scott, Inc. (P)

Shissler, Barbara. 1965. *Sports and Games in Art*. Minneapolis: Lerner Publishing Co. (U)

Smith, William Jay. 1962. *What Did I See?* New York: Crowell, Collier Press and MacMillan, Inc. (P)

Strache, Wolf. 1956. *Forms and Patterns in Nature*. New York: Pantheon Books, Inc. (U)

Swinton, William Elgin. 1961. *The Wonderful World of Prehistoric Animals*. New York: Garden City Books. (U)

Weisgard, Leonard. 1956. *Treasures To See*. New York: Harcourt Brace Jovanovich, Inc. (A)

Weiss, Harvey. 1956. *Clay, Wood and Wire*. New York: William R. Scott, Inc. (U)

——. 1958. *Paper, Ink and Roller*, New York: William R. Scott, Inc. (U)

——. 1961. *Pencil, Pen and Brush*. New York: William R. Scott, Inc. (U)

——. 1962. *Sticks, Spools and Feathers*. New York: William R. Scott, Inc. (U)

——. 1964. *Ceramics from Clay to Kiln*. New York: William R. Scott, Inc. (U)

——. 1966. *Paint, Brush and Palette*. New York: William R. Scott, Inc. (U)

Some excellent books on crafts for the teacher of art are the colorful Sunset Hobby and Craft Books. See the paperbacks on *Leather, Macrame, Stitchery & Patchwork, Ceramics and Weaving. Lane Publishing Co. Menlo Park, Calif. 94025*

Wolff, Janet, and Owett, Bernard. 1963. *Let's Imagine Colors.* New York: E. P. Dutton and Co., Inc. (A)

Wolff, Robert J. 1968. *Feeling Blue, Seeing Red, Hello, Yellow!* New York: Charles Scribner's Sons. (A)

Ylla. 1969. *Whose Eye Am I?* New York: Harper and Row, Publishers. (A)

Young, Mary. 1962. *Singing Windows.* (The Stained Glass Wonders of Chartres) New York: Abingdon Press. (U)

Zuelke, Ruth. 1964. *The Horse in Art.* Minneapolis: Lerner Publishing Co. (U)

Highly recommended for the children's art library are the following books by Shirley Glubok. Published by Atheneum and by MacMillan, New York.

The Art of Ancient Egypt
The Art of the Etruscans
The Art of Ancient Greece
The Art of Ancient Rome
The Art of the Lands of the Bible
The Art of India
The Art of Africa
The Art of Ancient Mexico
The Art of the Eskimo
The Art of the North American Indian
The Art of Ancient Peru
Art and Archeology

A richly complex still-life arrangement inspired this beautifully delineated crayon engraving by an upper grade child.

BOOKS FOR THE TEACHER

Alkema, Chester Jay. 1971. *Guide to Creative Art for Young People*. New York: Sterling Publishing Co. Inc.

Berenson, Paulus. 1972. *Finding One's Way With Clay*. New York: Simon and Schuster.

Cole, Natalie, 1966. *Children's Arts From Deep Down Inside*. New York: The John Day Co. Inc.

Faulkner, Ray and Ziegfeld, Edwin. 1963. *Art Today*. New York: Holt, Rinehart and Winston, Inc.

Gaitskell, Charles D., and Hurwitz, Al. 1974. *Children and Their Art*. New York: Harcourt Brace Jovanovich, Inc.

Herberholz, Donald W., and Herberholz, Barbara. 1969. *A Child's Pursuit of Art*. Dubuque, Iowa: William C. Brown Co.

Lansing, Kenneth. 1969. *Art, Artists and Art Education*. New York: McGraw-Hill Book Co.

Linderman, Earl W., and Herberholz, Donald W. 1964. *Developing Artistic and Perceptual Awareness*. Dubuque, Iowa: William C. Brown Co.

Lowenfeld, Viktor, and Brittain, W. L. 1964. *Creative and Mental Growth*. New York: The Macmillan Co.

McFee, June King. 1961. *Preparation for Art*. Belmont, California: Wadsworth.

Ocvirk, Otto G., Bone Robert O., Stinson, Robert E. and Wigg, Philip. 1975. *Art Fundamentals*. Dubuque, Iowa: William C. Brown Co.

Schinneller, James. 1969. *Art: Search and Self-Discovery*. Worcester, Massachusetts: Davis Publishers.

Wachowiak, Frank, and Hodge, David. 1971. *Art in Depth: A Qualitative Art Program for the Young Adolescent*. New York: Thomas Y. Crowell Co., Inc.

Top and center: *Paper plates came in handy for these yarn projects. No two are exactly alike! Macon, Georgia.* Bottom: *primary grade children used basic stitches and appliqué for these delightful radiating designs. Winona, Minnesota.*

appendix

D

AUDIOVISUAL AIDS

FILMS

The letter in parentheses following each film indicates whether suitable for primary grades (P) upper grades (U), or all grades (A). All films are 16 mm, sound and in color. Other letters refer to distributors whose addresses follow.

A Boy Creates (A) EBF
Animal Habitats (A) BFA
Around My Way New York City as seen through children's drawings (U)   CON/McGRAW
Art in Motion Color and design in motion. (U) EBF
Art and Perception: Learning to See (A) BFA
Arts and Crafts in West Africa (U) BFA
Arts and Crafts of Mexico (U) EBF
Artist and Nature (U) IFB
Art in Our World (U) BFA
Art in Action with Dong Kingman Contemporary watercolorist (U) HAR
Art—What Is It? Why Is It? (U) EBF

Top: *Linoleum Print. Grade 5.* Bottom: *Clay figure. Play ball! Grade 2. Japan.*

Batik Rediscovered (U) BFA

Begone Dull Care Color patterns set to music (A) IFB

Behind the Scenes of a Museum A Visit to Chicago's Natural History Museum (U) IFB

Birds and Etching Simple engraving process, (A) BFA

Birds in the City (A) BFA

Buma: African Sculpture Speaks (U) EBF

Butterfly Complete life cycle of swallow tail butterfly (A) BFA

Children Are Creative Children in art activities (U) BFA

Children Who Draw Japanese children drawing and painting (A) BRAN

Color in Clay (U) EBF

Crayon Resist (A) BFA

Creating with Clay (U) BFA

Creating with Paper (A) BFA

Design to Music Children painting as mood music is played (A) IFB

Discovering Art Series: Color; Composition; Creative Pattern; Dark and Light; Form in Art; Harmony in Art; Ideas for Art; Line; Texture (U) BFA

Dots Abstract designs set to music (A) IFB

Dream of Wild Horses (U) CON/McGRAW

Eskimo Arts and Crafts (U) IFB

Farm Babies and Their Mothers (P) BFA

Fiddle Dee Dee Art abstractions with sprightly violin music accompaniment (A) IFB

Human Figure in Art (U) BFA

Indian Ceremonials (U) SF

Insects and Painting Children use natural motifs as inspiration for art. (A) BFA

Introduction to Sculpture Methods Five sculptors at work in their studios. (U) BFA

Introduction to Contour Drawing (U) BFA

Introduction to Gesture Drawing (U) BFA

Introduction to Drawing Materials (U) BFA

Japanese Handicrafts (U) BFA

Lascaux: Cradle of Man's Art A look at the prehistoric cave paintings. (A) IFB

Look at That! Basic art elements through the eyes of two second grades (P) BFA

Loon's Necklace Tribal legend illustrated with North Pacific Indian masks (U) EBF

Make a Mobile (U) BFA

Masks A world collection of masks is shown (A) BFA

Monotype Prints Simple printmaking process for primary grades (P) IFB

Mural on Our Street (U) CON/McGRAW

Night in a Pet Shop (A) CON/McGRAW

Picture in Your Mind (U) IFB

Print with a Brayer (U) BFA

Rag Tapestry (U) IFB

Rhythm and Movement in Art (U) BFA

Sources of Art (U) BFA

Sun Symbol in Art (A) BFA

The Day the Colors Went Away (P) EBF

Torn Paper Simple torn paper techniques (A) IFB

Totems Tree carvings by Indians of British Columbia (U) IFB

Trip to the Moon Children of many countries paint their interpretations of a moon shot (U) BRAN

Watts Towers Simon Rodia's fantastic mosaic structures in Watts, California (U) CFS

Weeds and Mosaics Simple collage techniques utilizing found natural objects (U) BFA

What Is Art? (U) EBF

What Shall We Paint? (U) BFA

Working with Watercolor (U) IFB

Zoo Families (P) BFA

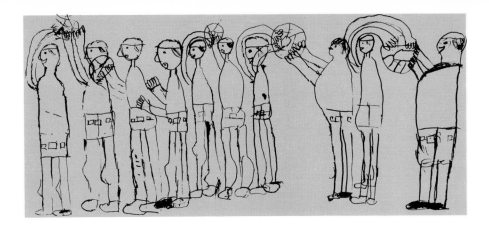

COLOR REPRODUCTIONS SOURCES

Harry N. Abrams
110 East 59th Street
New York, N.Y. 10022

Art Education, Inc.
Blauvelt, N.Y. 10913

Artext Prints, Inc.
Westpost, Conn. 06880

Associated American Artists,
Inc.
663 Fifth Avenue
New York, N.Y. 10022

New York Graphic Society
140 Greenwich Avenue
Greenwich, Conn 06830

Shorewood Reproductions,
Inc.
724 Fifth Avenue
New York, N.Y. 10019

World Publishing Co. (Skira)
2231 West 110th Street
Cleveland, Ohio 44102

E. Weyhe
794 Lexington Avenue
New York, N.Y. 10021

COLOR SLIDE AND FILMSTRIP SOURCES

American Library Color Slide
Co., Inc.
305 East 45th Street
New York, N.Y. 10017

Dr. Block Color Reproduc-
tions
1309 North Genesee Avenue
Los Angeles, California 90046

International Film Bureau
332 South Michigan Avenue
Chicago, Illinois 60604

McGraw Hill Book Co.
1221 Avenue of the Americas
New York, N.Y. 10020

Museum of Modern Art
Library
11 West 53rd Street
New York, N.Y. 10019

National Gallery of Art
Constitution Avenue and 6th
Street N.W.
Washington D.C. 20001

College and university instructors of art education courses as well as elementary art consultants may be interested in learning that two color filmstrips based on Emphasis Art *projects as well as two new filmstrips on* Japanese Child Art *edited by the author are now available from International Film Bureau, Inc. 332 South Michigan Ave., Chicago, Illinois.*

Dr. Konrad Prothman
2378 Soper Avenue
Baldwin, N.Y. 11510

Sandak, Inc.
4 East 48th Street
New York, N.Y. 10017

Art Institute of Chicago
South Michigan Avenue
Chicago, Illinois 60603

Society for Visual Education,
  Inc.
1345 Diversey Parkway
Chicago, Illinois 60614

FILM DISTRIBUTORS

BFA	BFA Educational Media, 11559 Santa Monica Boulevard, Los Angeles, Calif. 90025
BRAN	Brandon Films, Inc., 221 West 57th Street, New York, N.Y. 10019
EBF	Encyclopedia Brittanica Films, 425 N. Michigan Avenue, Chicago, Ill. 60611
HAR	Harmon Foundations, 140 Nassau Street, New York, N.Y. 10038
IFB	International Film Bureau, Inc., 332 South Michigan Avenue, Chicago, Ill. 60604
SF	Santa Fe Film Bureau, 80 East Jackson Boulevard, Chicago, Ill. 60604

Below: *These beautifully composed found materials collages by upper grade students, Atlanta, Georgia, show how enthusiastically youngsters respond to subjects and themes which interest them and with which they can identify. Bicycles and motorcycles are certainly part of their everyday life.*

appendix

E

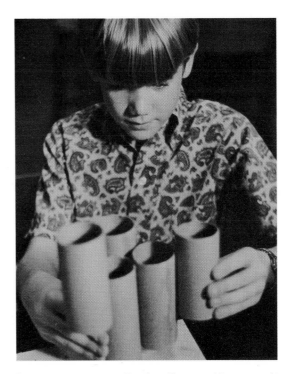

ART MATERIALS

To develop confidence that will help them teach art successfully in the elementary schools teachers must learn to be familiar with the art materials and tools that are commonly available to children in public schools. They should discover the creative potential of these materials through actual involvement with them. For example, if they have never experienced using ordinary wax crayons in a rich, brilliant way, then they will not be as enthusiastic or as effective in inspiring the children to see the crayon's multiple possibilities.

The following art materials and tools are generally provided in elementary schools today. Teachers should learn to identify them, use them, know the quality brands, discover available sources, order them in economy lots and sizes, and store them properly.

Top: *Linoleum print. Grade 5.* Bottom: *Youngsters' imaginations are challenged when they recycle found objects and discards into* *new configurations. Another instance where the whole is greater than the sum of its parts.*

EXPENDABLE MATERIALS

Pencils
Crayons
Fingerpaint
Tempera paint (poster paint, liquid or powder)
Watercolors in tins
Colored chalk
Cream manila paper
White drawing paper
Poster paper (assorted colors, lighter in weight than
    construction paper)
Construction paper (assorted colors)
Oak tag paper (tagboard)
School paste (glue, wheat paste)
School chalk
Clay

NONEXPENDABLE SUPPLIES, TOOLS

Easel brushes
Watercolor brushes
Scissors
Compasses
Rulers
Hammers, saws
Paper cutter
Stapler

Schools with more generous budgets often provide these supplementary art supplies and tools:

Oil pastels
Art gum erasers
Felt-nib pens

Printing inks (water base)
Felt marker watercolors
Elmer's Glue, Wilhold
Shellac
Rubber cement
India ink
Linoleum
Linoleum cutting tools
Brayers (rubber rollers for printmaking)
Wire
Clay glazes
Clay kiln
Tissue paper (assorted colors)

SOME PRACTICAL HINTS

Keep all art tools and materials in order. Store them in cigar boxes, shoe boxes, plastic freezer containers, or coffee or vegetable shortening tins. Label the containers. Paint tools with an identifying color.

Keep all tools clean. Do not allow metal tools to get rusty. Wipe them dry if they become moist and oil or grease them if they are to be stored for a period of time. Do not use scissors for clay or plaster projects! Never pour wet plaster down the sink or drain! Scrape excess wet plaster into newspaper-lined waste containers.

Mount motivational resource photographs on oak tag or tagboard and store in labeled accordion folders, or put in plastic loose leaf protectors and keep in notebook binders.

Wash brushes clean (use detergent, if necessary) and store with bristle ends up in a jar or coffee can.

Be sure youngsters rinse and clean watercolor tins. Leave them open and stack them to dry out overnight. Order semimoist cakes of watercolor in bulk to refill empty watercolor tins.

Store scrap construction paper and tissue paper flat in drawers or discarded blanket boxes. This helps prevent the paper from being crushed.

When placing orders for tempera or poster colors in liquid or powder form, always order more white paint. Children use a lot of white to mix tints or lighter colors. You can also order white, black, and colored crayons or oil pastels in bulk.

Beaver board, or Upson board (a heavy, cream-colored laminated cardboard available in 4 × 8 foot or 4 × 10 foot pieces in ¼ inch thickness) is excellent for drawing boards and for working surfaces on desks. Have the lumber dealer cut the board for you into 18 × 24 inch sections. For longer wear, mask-tape the edges of the drawing boards.

Yarn purchased on skeins can be rewound on balls or spools for ready use. A closed cardboard carton with holes punched in it for the yarn ends makes an excellent dispenser.

Keep school paste in the jar until ready to use, then dispense on small pieces of tagboard or cardboard. Scrape off unused paste at end of period into jar, moisten slightly with a few drops of water, then cap tightly.

When crayons break and do not fit easily into the original package, have children store them in quart coffee or vegetable shortening cans or half-gallon waxed milk cartons, cut down as needed.

Powdered tempera is, of course, much easier to store than the liquid kind, but liquid tempera has definite advantages. It is always ready to use if sealed securely. The most vexing problem in tempera usage is deciding what to do with unused liquid tempera left in muffin tins, plastic egg cartons, or TV Dinner trays. It is almost impossible to pour it back into the original container. That is why paint should be doled out a small amount at a time with refills as needed. Usually the teacher should be in charge of paint distribution. Before closing covers on tempera jars, check plasticity of the paint. If it is too dry, add a few drops of water to ensure moistness. Cap tightly. To prevent paint from becoming sour, add a few drops of wintergreen or oil of cloves to each container.

RECYCLING FOUND MATERIALS

When elementary school teachers consider supplies for art activities, they usually think first in terms of those materials that are available in the commercial art market. In today's productive world, however, there are a number of other sources they can tap, among them the discarded or junked everyday items, empty containers, scraps, remnants, and hundreds of things ordinarily thought of as worthless but that, with a little imagination and ingenuity, can be recycled into the art program.

Most of the items listed below can be found in basements, attics, garages, alleys, junkyards, department store disposal areas, and wastebaskets. Children and their parents should be enlisted in the campaign to build a store of such discarded materials for use in classroom projects. Found objects can definitely enrich and expand the elementary art program especially when the school is operating on a limited budget. Care must be taken however that the found objects do not end up in lost efforts. Selection, discrimination and restraint must be employed so that the "whole construction becomes much more than just the sum of its parts."

baby food jars
bags, paper
balloons
balls, rubber, Styrofoam
balls, Ping Pong
bark (tree)
beads
blades (broken saw)
blinds (matchstick)
blotters
bolts and nuts
bones
book jackets
bottles
boxes (cigar)
boxes (oatmeal)
buckles
bulbs (electric)
bulbs (photo flash)
buttons
candles
cans (tin)
caps (bottles)
cards (game)
carpet samples
cartons (egg)
cartons (milk)
cartons (ice cream)
cellulose sponges
celotex

checkers
clock parts
cloth remnants
clothes pins
coils (old)
cones (fir)
cones (paper)
confetti
cord
corks
dominoes
driftwood
feathers
felt pieces
foam rubber pieces
foil (aluminum)
fur
gourds
keys
leather scraps
linoleum scraps
magazines
marbles
masonite pieces
meat trays (plastic)
mirrors
nails
newspapers
paper plates, trays
paper towels

paper (shelf)
paper (gift wrap)
pegboard pieces
pins
pipe cleaners
plywood scraps
polish (shoe)
Q-tips
reed
ribbon, ric rac
rope
rubber (innertube)
sandpaper
screws
seashells
shades (window)
shingles

sponge (metal, plastic)
spools (thread)
sticks (applicator)
sticks (pickup)
straws (wax, cellophane, paper)
tile (acoustic)
tile (vinyl)
tissue paper (colored)
tongue depressors
toothbrush
toothpicks
tubes (mailing)
TV dinner trays
wallpaper samples
wood scraps
x-ray plates (used)
yarn

SOME SPECIAL MATERIALS AND TOOLS: SUGGESTED USES

Beaverboard (Upsonboard)	For drawing or sketching boards, desk of table tops. Mural surfaces. Protect edge of board with masking tape.
Brayer (rubber roller)	For inking plate in printmaking. Obtain the sturdy *soft rubber* brayer for longer wear
Dextrin (powdered)	Add to dry or moist clay (5% to 10%) and finished piece will harden without firing in kiln.
Firebrick (porous, insulation)	For upper-grade carving projects.
Grog	Aggregate for plaster molds, clay conditioner
Masonite (tempered)	For clay modeling surfaces, inking surfaces, in printmaking, rinsing board for tempera resists.
Pariscraft	Plaster-impregnated gauze in varied widths for additive sculpture projects.
Plaster (molding)	For plaster reliefs, sculpture.
Polystyrene	For printmaking plates, craft projects, simple printing pieces.
Posterboard (railroad board)	For multicrayon engraving surface.
Rub'n'Buff	Metallic and colored paste to use as patina on sculpture, plaster, and aluminum foil reliefs, ceramics.
Shreddimix	Prepared mixture for papier mâché projects.
Shellacol	Solvent for cleaning shellac brushes.
Sloyd knife (Hyde)	All purpose utility knife with a 2 inch semisharp blade excellent for carving in plaster, for crayon engraving.
Transfer paper	A white transfer paper for use in tracing preliminary sketches in crayon engraving projects.
Treasure Gold	Metallic and colored paste to use as patinas on plaster sculpture and on plaster and aluminum foil reliefs.
X-acto knife	Craft knife with sharp interchangeable blades for cutting cardboard. *CAUTION: to be used by teacher only.*

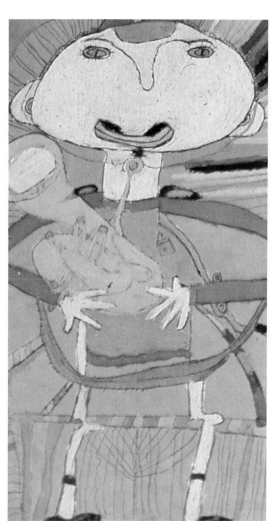
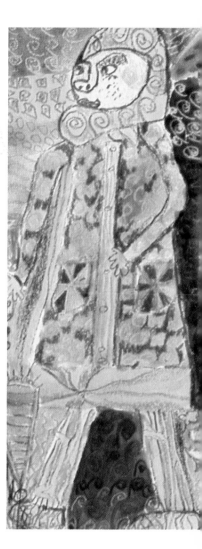

The human figure expressed and interpreted in a variety of art media. Beginning at left: Mixed media, tempera, oil pastel, and crayon-watercolor resist. Intermediate grades.

appendix

F

FACILITIES FOR ART

THE CLASSROOM AS ART ROOM

The elementary classroom or the art room can be the child's first and often most enduring art lesson. It is here, through exciting displays and eye-catching exhibits, that the teacher can provide the example for a creative, inspiring, and stimulating environment. Certainly the students should be invited to involve themselves in projects that will help make the room attractive and colorful. Bulletin boards and displays should be changed often and regularly to provide evaluative opportunities for completed projects and to whet interest for further endeavors. Still-life arrangements should be in view for sketching and painting purposes. Students should be encouraged to contribute to the store of found objects and nature's forms on constant display in the classroom.

Here are some ideas for creating interest in the art class and providing subject matter for art:

Hang a number of open umbrellas from the ceiling. They may overlap each other. The more variety the better. Oriental umbrellas are especially colorful. Also try Japanese, Chinese, and Indian kites, balloons, and banners. Caution: Don't hang these from light fixtures.

Top: *Linoleum print. Grade 3.* Bottom: *Found objects were employed to give decorative detail to this clay elephant.*

When nothing else is available for a still-life arrangement, stack a bunch of chairs or stools on top of each other—some sticking out at different angles. For more interest weave some drapery material in and out of the openings. You might suggest that the older students paint the negative shapes first as a possible design approach.

Drape different kinds of fabric, plain and patterned, against a bulletin board—pin the material so you have bunches or knots of cloth balanced by drapery swaggers. Pin some old hats against the drapery. This makes an excellent study for color compositions.

Bring into the classroom a fairly large dead tree branch. Mount it against a light-colored wall or bulletin board. It provides an unmatched subject inspiration for contour or linear drawing projects and is also excellent for display of papier mâché birds or paper sculpture butterflies, fish, etc.

Have students remove their shoes and stack them in the middle of table or on a chair for a still-life arrangement. If they object to this, have them bring an extra pair of shoes or boots to use in the still life. Shoes, boots, hats, caps, jackets, and gloves provide interesting, organic shapes for drawing because they conform to the human form.

Arrange bottles of different colored glass on window sills. Fill some of them with dried weeds or branches, some with colored water, and others with strips of aluminum foil. Bleached animal bones make excellent studies for line drawings and value interpretations. Also use them as inspiration for clay modeled forms.

Build a color environment as a motivation for painting. Make it a class "happening." Have students collect colored tissue paper, crepe paper, colorful fabrics, yarns, ribbons, confetti, gift wrap paper, balloons, party hats in all colors and fluorescent Day-glo materials. If you arrange the display near a window you can incorporate colored cellophane and plastics as well.

Large potted plants of assorted foliages and blossoms make excellent sketching and painting subject themes. They also give life to a room, especially in those schools where air conditioning has unfortunately made the windowless classroom an architectural necessity.

Keep on hand some large colorful pieces of fabric, shawls, old bedspreads, and blankets to use as drapery on class models and in still-life arrangements. Students respond more readily to costumed models and unusual backgrounds. Set up an exciting still life against a wall, then pose a student or students in costume against it. The models may be standing, sitting, or reclining. Have students take turns modeling.

Contact or write travel agencies here and abroad to secure large colorful travel posters of various countries. Display these in the classroom for an eye-catching effect.

The qualitative art program in the elementary school depends, in part, on adequate and functional instructional facilities. Some schools boast a multipurpose art room, but the majority of elementary art experiences today take place in the self-contained classroom. This often places a limitation on the variety of art activities that can be programmed. However, if certain minimal and vital art facility requirements are met in the plans of the classrooms still to be constructed, the climate for growth in art in tomorrow's elementary schools will be a more favorable one. Basically the changes that need to be made are in the strategic areas of storage, display, and cleanup facilities.

LOCATION

If a multipurpose art room is planned, it should be preferably on the first or ground floor, adjacent to the stage of the auditorium or to the cafeteria and near a service entrance. An outdoor court, easily accessible from the art room, can provide excellent auxiliary space for sketching, mural making, ceramics, constructions, and sculptural projects in favorable weather.

SPACE ALLOTMENT

Sufficient space should be provided to allow students to work on individual projects with some flexibility of movement, to permit rearrangement of furniture for group projects, and to ensure a regular flow of student traffic to storage, display, and cleanup areas or stations.

The self-contained classroom should be planned to provide adequate space at the rear of the room and along one or two walls for storage, cleanup (sink) facility, and counter or surface working areas. There should be sufficient room at the rear of the class for one or more large tables suitable for group projects and special craft activities.

FURNITURE

In both the self-contained classroom or the special art room, desk and table surfaces of nonglare, waterproof, and scratch-resistant material are recommended. White or light-colored Formica working surfaces have many advantages but they must be protected during projects involving cutting or hammering. Tables and desks should be adjustable for height and easily movable to provide for group or project activities. In the multipurpose art room, stools which can be recessed under tables can ease the traffic problem. In the primary-level classrooms freestanding easels can effectively augment the limited table and desk painting surface.

STORAGE

Effective storage facilities are a definite asset in expediting a multiproject art program. There should be adequate storage for art supplies, tools, visual aids, work in process, and completed art projects reserved for display.

Supply storage should be provided for assorted art papers (drawers or slots should have inside measurements slightly larger than the size of the paper itself); tempera or poster paint, watercolors, oil pastels, crayons, inks, and paste (adjustable shelves are recommended for these supplies); yarn, wood, found materials, and clay (bin type storage, tote-tray cabinet, mobile metal-lined clay cart, galvanized or heavy plastic waste containers, large cardboard cartons painted in bright colors).

A cabinet or movable cart with shelves and panels is suggested for small tool storage. A simple pegboard panel attached to a wall and the necessary accompanying hardware will alleviate the most pressing tool storage problems. Painting an identifying shape or outline of each tool on the panel will help expedite storage and provide a ready inventory of tools.

Since so much of the children's art centers around painting, there should be adequate horizontal storage spaces for painting projects in process. This is especially true in the special art room where one class follows another and painting stations must be cleared quickly. There are some excellent horizontal storage facilities on the market but too often the budget does not allow for their purchase. A simple yet effective flatwork storage unit can be constructed of a strong framework of 2 × 4's and ¾-inch plywood and pull-out shelves of masonite, plywood, or ⅜-inch Upsonboard. A clothesline and spring clothespins can be used as a drying facility for in-process and completed vegetable, cardboard, or linoleum prints.

A critical problem in the self-contained classroom is the storage of three-dimensional projects in progress such as clay sculpture or pottery, paper sculpture, **papier-mâché** or box constructions, stabiles, and mobiles. Counter space above storage cabinets, the floor along a wall, and closet shelves are some possibilities. Tote trays provide another solution. Mobiles in process or on display could be suspended from a wire line strung from the tops of doors and windows. Avoid hanging mobiles and other constructions from light fixtures or light baffles. This practice may prove hazardous and damaging.

Illustrations on this page show easily constructed storage facilities for both flat work and three-dimensional projects. The plastic tote trays are commercially available.

CLEANUP FACILITIES

In order to minimize traffic problems, sinks should be easily accessible from all parts of the classroom. They should not be located in a closet or a corner of the room. They should be stainproof and easily cleaned. Multiple mixing faucets, heavy duty drains, and sink traps are recommended. Sinks should be large enough to allow several youngsters to use them at the same time. They should be low enough so that the children can reach them with ease; if not, they should be provided with step-up platforms. For special art rooms a peninsula or island sink is recommended.

DISPLAY FACILITIES

A generous amount of space should be allotted for display purpose and for instructional bulletin boards. This holds true for either the special art room or the self-contained classroom. Display and exhibition panel backgrounds should be neutral in color. Subtle nonglare whites, grays, and blacks are recommended. Surfaces, in most instances, should be matte finish utilizing easy pinning or stapling material such as cork or celotex. Random-punch butt-end acoustic tile can be glued directly to wall surfaces or to masonite panels to form a simple, yet effective, display facility. Cork-surfaced doors on cupboards and storage cabinets will augment the display possibilities. In the newest art rooms cork display panels from floor to ceiling are being installed. It is advisable in future school planning to designate one classroom wall entirely for display or mural-making surfaces.

A sixth grade youngster sketches from still-life arrangement using school chalk on colored construction paper. See completed oil pastel composition on page 247.

OTHER SPECIFICATIONS

Floors should be of nonskid material, hard, yet resilient and easily cleaned. Neutral colored asphalt or plastic tile is recommended. Ceilings should be acoustically treated and of a color that provides maximum light reflection. Lighting should be of sufficient kilowatt intensity to provide students with adequate light and minimum glare. Room-darkening shades or blinds should be installed to expedite the showing of color slides and films. White-surfaced slate boards can aid effectively in presenting art lessons in a more realistic context. These boards can also serve as screens for slide and film projection. Electric outlets should be provided at intervals around the classroom. Check with the electrician on voltage needed especially if a clay or enamel kiln is to be installed. Electrical outlets should not be positioned adjacent to sink areas.

SPECIAL EQUIPMENT

Whether in the self-contained classroom or the art room, special furniture and equipment can often be a deciding factor in implementing the program. The following items are generally recommended: clay bin or cart, vibrating jig saw, heavy-duty clothes wringer, color-slide projector, projection screen, workbench with vises, large-size paper cutter, electric heating plate, utility cart, ceramic kiln, metal enameling kiln, free-standing easels, drying rack for flat work in progress, gun tacker, stapler.

Fish mobile. Top: *Drawing on butcher or Kraft paper. When completed a second matching shape is cut out.* Center: *Painting the two sides of the fish. Both painted fish should be facing opposite directions to assemble correctly. When paint is dry partially staple fish, fill with crushed newspapers and staple closed.* Bottom: *Mobile displayed in classroom.*

appendix

G

GLOSSARY

Analogous colors—colors closely related, neighbors on the color wheel or spectrum: green, blue-green, yellow-green, for example.

Appliqué—decorative design made by cutting pieces of one material and applying them by gluing or stitching to the surface of another materials.

Armature—framework (of wood, wire, etc.) used to support constructions of clay, papier mâché, or plaster.

Balsa—strong, lightweight wood used for construction and model building.

Baren—a device made of cardboard and dried leaf which is used as a hand press to make a print by rubbing.

Batik—a method of designing on fabric by sealing with melted wax those areas not to be dyed.

Beaverboard—a light, semirigid construction board of compressed wood pulp. Used for lightweight drawing boards, cardboard construction, etc. Also sold as *Upsonboard*.

Bisque—clay in its fired or baked state.

Brayer—rubber roller used for inking in printmaking projects.

Burnish—to make smooth or shiny by a rubbing or polishing action.

Top: *Woodblock print. Grade 4. Japan.* Bottom: *Only in clay could a young child capture the inimitable quality of this delightfully whimsical figure. Grade 2.*

Ceramic—a word used to describe clay construction and products.

Charcoal—drawing stick or pencil made from blackened, charred wood.

Chipboard—heavy cardboard, usually gray in color, in varying thicknesses, used for collage, collograph, and construction projects.

Color—an element of art.

Collage—composition made by arranging and gluing materials to a flat surface.

Collograph—a print made from a collage surface plate utilizing an assortment of papers, cardboards, string, etc.

Complementary colors—colors found opposite each other on the color wheel: yellow and violet, for example.

Contour drawing—a line drawing delineating the contours or edges of an object.

Construction paper—a strong, absorbent paper available in many colors, used for drawings, paintings, pastels, paper, sculpture, and collages.

Easel—a frame to support an artist's canvas.

Embossing—making a raised or relief design on metal or leather by tooling or indenting the surface.

Encaustic—a painting technique employing hot beeswax mixed with pigment. Sometimes used to describe melted crayon paintings.

Engraving—a process of incising or scratching into a hard surface to produce an image.

Findings—metal clasps, loops, etc. used in jewelry making.

Fire—in ceramics, to bake clay in a kiln.

Fixative—a commercial preparation in a spray form used to protect easily-smudged surfaces in chalk, pastel, or charcoal drawings (also fixatif).

Found objects—discards, remnants, driftwood, samples, and throwaways that are used in collages, constructions, as printmaking stamps, etc.

Frieze—a decorated, horizontal band along the upper part of a room.

Greenware—unfired clay when in leather-hard stage, firm but not fully dry.

Grout—a filler such as plaster rubbed in between clay or glass tesserae in a mosaic.

Glaze—a transparent or semitransparent coating of a color stain over a plain surface or other color.

Gum eraser—a soft eraser used in drawing available in cube or rectangular solid.

Hue—another word for "color."

India ink—a waterproof ink made from lampblack. Used for drawing, tempera resist, aluminum foil relief.

Kiln—an oven for drying, firing and glazing clay.

Kneaded eraser—a gray colored eraser that must be stretched and kneaded to be effective. For charcoal drawings.

Line—an element of art.

Loom—the supporting framework for the warp in weaving.

Macramé—lacework made by knotting and weaving cords into a pattern.

Manila paper—a general purpose drawing or crayoning paper, usually cream color.

Masonite—a pressed board made of wood fibers. Used for clay-modeling boards, inking surfaces in printmaking, etc.

Mat board—a heavy poster board used for mounting or matting pictures. (available in many colors and textures)

Mobile—a free-moving construction in space.

Monoprint—one-of-a-kind print. Usually impression is made on inked glass plate.

Mosaic—a design or composition made by arranging and pasting tesserae or cut out shapes of material next to each other on a background surface.

Mural—a monumental painting, usually painted directly on a wall or side of a building. May also be executed in paper, metal, or clay.

Newsprint paper—newspaper stock. Used for sketches or preliminary drawings.

Oil pastel—a kind of pastel for coloring. Combines qualities of both chalk and oil.

Patina—a word sometimes used to describe the color of antiqued stains and glazes on metals, ceramics, and plaster reliefs.

Papier mâché—name given to paper crafts utilizing newsprint paper moistened with wallpaper paste or laundry starch.

Pattern—design made by repeating a motif or symbol.

Perspective—the creation of a three dimensional visual illusion on a two-dimensional surface by means of converging lines and diminishing sizes of objects.

Plaster—a white, powdery substance, which, when mixed with water, forms a quick-setting molding or casting material. Sometimes called Plaster of Paris (also moulding plaster).

Positive-Negative—*Positive* shapes in a composition or painting are the solid objects, the people, trees, buildings, etc. *Negative* shapes are the unoccupied or empty spaces between the positive shapes.

Primary colors—red, yellow, blue. Three basic hues.

Radiation—lines, shapes, or color emanating from a central point of interest.

Relief—a projection of something from a surface. Shallow relief as in a coin. Used to describe plaster relief.

Repoussé—a metal work in which the design is tooled or hammered into a relief form.

Rubber cement—a clean, quick-drying latex type of cement or glue. For paper work.

Scoring (clay)—to make grooves in clay using an edged tool, as a step in cementing two parts of clay together. Also used to describe the guiding indent in paper sculpture folding.

Secondary colors—green, orange, violet. Achieved by mixing primary colors.

Selvedge—the edge of the fabric where the weft returns to weave its way to the opposite edge.

Shade—refers to the darker values of a color. Maroon is a shade of red.

Shellac—a kind of lacquer used to seal and protect certain art projects. Clear shellac is generally recommended.

Shellac thinner—a solvent for shellac. (Shellacol, methanol, alcohol.) For cleaning shellac brushes.

Slip—clay thinned with water to a creamy consistency. Used as binder between two pieces of clay when modeling. Slip, colored or white, called engobe, can be used to decorate greenware.

Sketch—usually a preliminary drawing made with pencil, pen, chalk, crayon charcoal, etc.

Stabile—a construction in space usually with no moving parts. Also space modulator.

Still life—an arrangement of objects usually on a table as a subject for drawing, painting, etc.

Tagboard—sometimes called oak tag. A shiny-coated, pliable cardboard used in collage, collographs, glue line prints, and constructions.

Tempera paint—an opaque, water-soluble paint. Available in liquid or powder form. Also called showcard or poster paint.

Tessera—small piece of material (paper, ceramic, vinyl, etc.) fitted and glued to a surface to make a mosaic. (Plural, tesserae.)

Texture—the actual and/or visual feel of a surface; for example, bark on a tree, fur on an animal.

Tint—refers to the lighter values of a color. Pink is a tint of red.

Value—in color, the lightness or darkness of the hue.

Watercolors—watersoluble colors. Usually transparent or semitransparent. Available in semimoist cakes or tubes.

Warp—the thread or yarn that supports the weft.

Wedging—a method of preparing clay by kneading and squeezing it to expel the air pockets and make it more plastic.

Weft—the thread or other material that goes across the warp from side to side.

INDEX

Aluminum foil relief, 173–175
Animals, drawing, 95–100
Art appreciation, 46, 68–71
Art fundamentals, 11–21
Art materials, 232–237
Art vocabulary
  grades one and two, 52
  grades three and four, 59
  grades five and six, 64
Audiovisual aids, 37–38, 68–71, 228–231

Balance, 13, 18, 91
Bas reliefs, 39
Batiks, 39
  tempera-india ink, 109–112
Blind contour drawing, 55
Box sculpture, 204–209

Cardboard prints, *see* Collographs
Carving, *see* Sculpture
Casting, 39

Centricity, 18
Ceramics, 39, 190
  grades one and two, 51–52
  grades three and four, 58
  grades five and six, 63–64
Chalkboard instructions, 34
Children, characteristics of
  grades one and two, 217–218
  grades three and four, 218
  grades five and six, 219
Classroom facilities, 33, 238–243
  cleanup facilities, 242
  display facilities, 242–243
  furniture, 230
  location, 240
  space allotment, 240
  special equipment, 243
  storage, 240–241
Clay, 183–189
  figure modeling, 63–64, 70
  grades one and two, 51–52

Clay (*continued*)
  grades three and four, 58
  grades five and six, 63–64
  patch techniques, 64
  plaster relief and, 191–193
  relief, 186, 188–189
Cleanup facilities in classroom, 242
Collage, 146–149
  grades one and two, 50–51
  grades three and four, 56–57
  grades five and six, 63
  tissue paper, 150–152
Collographs (cardboard relief print), 51, 57, 63, 166–171, 190
Color, 5, 13, 15–17
  neutralization, 16, 56
  theories, 16
  washes, 14
  wheel, 16
Color awareness
  grades one and two, 49–50
  grades three and four, 55–56
  grades five and six, 62–63
Constructions in space, 201–203
Continuity of learning, 45–65
Contour-drawing techniques, 54
Converging lines, 17, 86
Crayon, 39, 119–121
  encaustic, 39, 127–129
  engraving, 119, 131–133
  multicrayon engraving, 119, 135–136
  resist, 119, 123–125, 143
Crosshatching, 61

Decorative (flat) space, 17
Dedication, of teachers, 29
Designing
  grades one and two, 48–49
  grades three and four, 54–55
  grades five and six, 61–62

Display facilities in classroom, 242–243
Diversity, 18–20
Dominance, 13
Double pinch pots, 58, 64
Drawing, 71
  animals, 95–100
  blind contour, 55
  contour-drawing techniques, 54–55
  crayon encaustic, 39, 127–129
  crayon engraving, 119, 131–133
  crayon resist, 119, 123–125, 143
  figure, 74–84
  grades one and two, 48–49
  grades three and four, 54–55
  grades five and six, 61–62
  landscape, 85–88
  multicrayon engraving, 119, 135–136
  still-life, 89–94
  See also Painting

Environment, 23–27
Emphasis, 13, 18, 19
Expressionistic era, 17

Figure drawing, 74–84
Flowing ink, 14
Foreshortening, 17, 62
Form, 13
Formal (symmetrical) balance, 18
Found object print, 51, 57, 63
Fundamentals of art, 11–21
Furniture in classroom, 240

Geometric formula, 15
Glue line relief prints, 51, 57, 63, 163–165
Grades one and two
  art vocabulary, 52
  ceramics, 51–52
  characteristics of children, 217–218

Grades one and two (*continued*)
 collage, 50–51
 color awareness, 49–50
 drawing, designing, and painting, 48–49
 growth of children in art, 221–222
 printmaking, 51
 suggested subjects or themes, 53
Grades three and four
 art vocabulary, 59
 ceramics, 58
 characteristics of children, 218
 collage, 56–57
 color awareness, 55–56
 drawing, designing, and painting, 54–55
 growth of children in art, 223
 printmaking, 57–58
 suggested subjects or themes, 59–60
Grades five and six
 art vocabulary, 64
 ceramics, 63–64
 characteristics of children, 219
 collage, 63
 color awareness, 62–63
 drawing, designing, and painting, 61–62
 growth of children in art, 223
 printmaking, 63
 suggested subjects or themes, 65

Hatching, 61
Horizon levels, 17, 86

Impressionists, 17
Informal (asymmetrical) balance, 18
Instructions, chalkboard, 34
Intensity, 15
Interest, student, 40–41, 43
Introductory session, 33, 40

Landscape drawing, 85–88
Line, 5, 13–14

Linear image, 13
Linoleum block printing, 34, 63, 177–181, 190
Location of classroom, 240

Mask making, 71, 210–214
Materials, 232–237
Metal repoussé, 190
Monoprint, 57, 63
Mosaics, 39, 154–156
Motivation, 6, 37–43
Multicrayon engraving, 119, 135–136
Murals, 115–117

Negative shapes (spaces), 15, 17, 56, 61
Neutralization of color, 16, 56
Normal balance, 91

Oil pastel, 39, 139–141
Oil pastel resist, 143–144
Overlapping, 91

Painting, 69, 70
 box sculptures, 208–209
 grades one and two, 48–49
 grades three and four, 54–55
 grades five and six, 61–62
 oil pastel, 39, 139–141
 oil pastel resist, 143–144
 with tempera, 101–107
 See also Drawing
Palette, 16
Papier-mâché, 190
Pattern, 5, 13
Personal experiences as motivation, 38
Perspective, 17, 62, 86
Pinch pots, 51–52, 58
Planning, 33
Plaster, 190–193, 195–196
Plastic space, 17
Poetry, 2–4

Point, 13
Polystyrene sheet print, 57
Positive shapes, 15, 56, 61
Post and lintel process, 58, 188
Poster paint, 39
Postimpressionistic era, 17
Printmaking, 71
  aluminum foil relief, 173–175
  collographs, 51, 57, 63, 166–171, 190
  found object, 51, 57, 63
  glue line relief, 51, 57, 63, 163–165
  grades one and two, 51
  grades three and four, 57–78
  grades five and six, 63
  linoleum block, 34, 63, 177–181, 190
  monoprint, 57, 63
  polystyrene sheet, 57
  vegetable, 51, 57, 63, 158–161
Project evaluation, 41

Radiation, 13
Readings, recommended, 224–227
Recycling materials, 234–235
Repetition, 91
Rhythm-repetition, 13

Sculpture, 71
  box, 204–209
  clay, 183–189
  constructions in space, 201–203
  plaster relief, 190–193
  subtractive, 190, 195–198
  wire, 203
Shade, 15
Shading, 17, 61
Shape, 13, 14–15
Sketching field trips, 85–87
Slab containers, 64

Slip-cementing, 58
Smudging, 14
Space, 13, 17
Space allotment in classroom, 240
Space-in-depth, 17
Stereotypes, 6, 11, 38
Still-life drawing, 89–94
Stippling, 61
Stitchery, 190
Storage in classroom, 240–241
Student interest, 40–41, 43
Subordination, 13
Subtractive sculpture, 190, 195–198
Symmetry, see Balance

Teachers, role of, 5–6, 29–34
Tempera
  batik, 109–112
  painting with, 101–107
Tesserae, 154, 156
Texture, 5, 13
Time, budgeting of, 33
Tint, 15
Tissue paper, 39
  collage, 150–152
Totem poles, 214

Unity, 13

Value, 5, 13, 15, 61
Vanishing points, 17, 86
Variety, 13, 18–20, 91
Vegetable prints, 51, 57, 63, 158–161

Washes, 14, 61
Weaving, 190
Wire sculpture, 203

Printer and Binder: Kingsport Press
82   9   8   7